THIS IS MARRIAGE

DR. RICHARD JOSEPH KREJCIR

America Star Books

First printing

America Star Books has allowed this work to remain exactly as the author intended, verbatim, without editorial input.

All Scripture quotations, unless otherwise stated, are from The Holy Bible, "New International Version," (North American Edition) by Zondervan Bible Publishers © 1973, 1978, 1987 International Bible Society. Used by permission of Zondervan Publishing House.

Softcover 9781611022599
PUBLISHED BY AMERICA STAR BOOKS, LLLP
www.americastarbooks.com

Printed in the United States of America

Into Thy Word Ministries, Pasadena, California, USA
www.intothyword.org

Dedication

I dedicate this work to the GLORY OF OUR LORD!

To our God and Father be glory for ever and ever. Amen.
Philippians 4:20

Many thanks to all the people who have discipled and inspired me over the years. To name just a few: Robert B. Munger, Chuck Miller, R.C. Sproul, and, of course, my friend and mentor, Francis A. Schaeffer. A special thanks to my editors, Kristin and Fran, who have worked very hard on the manuscript, and to the people in my church and Bible Study who have encouraged, prayed, given me insights, and kept me sane on this journey.

My utmost dedication is to my great love with appreciation for all of her help—my wife, Mary Ruth. *"I found the one my heart loves."* Song of Solomon 3:4

For Christ's love compels us, because we are convinced that one died for all, and therefore all died. And he died for all, that those who live should no longer live for themselves but for him who died for them and was raised again. 2 Corinthians 5:14-15

CONTENTS

The real authenticity of our Lord will enable us to build a real authenticity of love and respect that will in turn build a "Wondrous Marriage!"

PREFACE

Love is a Verb; so is Marriage

God's precepts on building a great marriage and Biblical instruction on making marriage work and succeed—even in times of stress and turmoil.

However, each one of you also must love his wife as he loves himself, and the wife must respect her husband. Ephesians 5:33

The world tells you that it is all about you; your needs must be fulfilled. Marriage is about making me—yes, 'ME,'—happy! Look at all the excitement of the pursuit, the proposal, the engagement, the wedding plans and so forth. Jump ahead a year, two years or ten. What do you have? Do you have the thrill, the rush, the anticipation? For most, not so much. The fact is that seeking to be self-fulfilled did not work out so well.

Why? There are two of you in the marriage, and you cannot be fulfilled and happy if you do so at the other's expense; unfortunately, this can happen to the best of us, and it tends to happen over time. Blessedly, there is a solution to bring back that excitement, hope, and wonder. The Bible has a better plan, and the Bible gives all the instruction to make a marriage work—you can have a wondrous marriage! It is about understanding and applying what *love and marriage really is* to be about and the practice of *real* forgiveness. Of course, communication is important, too. If we do not know what marriage is supposed to be about and only focus on what we want it to be, we will fail. We will fail. If we refuse to know and practice real love, we will have only sadness and brokenness. If we are not willing to forgive, we have... nothing. We have nothing ahead, except broken expectations, disappointments, and hurts that create anger, bitterness, and a life of dysfunction ultimately ending in divorce or general unpleasantness!

Remember, though, you can have joy and real purpose in your marriage; you can escape a relationship rife with chaos and dysfunction. You and your spouse can have a successful marriage!

In this book, I will help guide you through the insights from God's Word. Love may be a noun as a word, as in a person, or place or thing; but, love is more of a call to action, to be—a verb, an action. Marriage is also is a verb—a call to action.

The efforts and guidance for this endeavor are based on the Word of God and learning and distilling from more than 20 years of research and 19 years of humbling practice. (Remember, you have no need to rely solely on what I say; look it up for yourselves in the Bible.) You can build a good marriage if you want to learn to love, respect, forgive, pray, and be humble in your relationship with Christ and with your spouse. You will succeed.

God tells us what makes a good marriage fun and enjoyable. This book aims to guide you, in Christ, to a wondrous marriage. The challenge in this book is for you who are already married and how to realize all the joy of a good marriage. If you are looking for advice and guidance about finding a potential spouse, I encourage you to still immerse yourself in God's Word and, perhaps, check out my book, "Healthy Relationships."

The ultimate goal of this book is to let you know that your marriage can be good. It can be fun. You and your spouse can be close best friends.

Unfortunately, many marriages don't seem to have this. I will not bore you with statistics, but over half of marriages are in trouble, and the rest, well only one eighth of those who are married consider both husband and wife to be happy. The rest—you and me—want better marriages, but we feel stuck, stagnant, even hopeless. They feel frustrated and hurt; they feel that maybe they've made a mistake and wish for a time machine, a do-over button, or a redo switch. Too many feel that fun, adventure, and happiness are in the past, but that is just not true. You can be close and grow closer together. Your marriage can be an exciting adventure that is meaningful and encouraging for both of you.

In fact, your marriage can be the best part of your life.

You perhaps are thinking, "What is the catch"? Okay, there is a bit of a catch. Like anything worthwhile and important, a good marriage requires work, commitment, and maintenance to be effectual. This book is about how to go about that. Like anything worth doing, you have to be willing to do it. You have to want a healthier marriage. You need to work on better communication. You do need to pray with one another. You have to know what it means to cherish and what it means to respect. You must learn what love is and what it is not. You have to see what God has for you, not just what you want. Finally, you must want it to get it.

Look at it like this. When you first started to drive, did you know what you know now? Are you a better driver now? I hope so. When you first started, I bet you thought you knew it all, you were so excited; you did not always listen to wise instruction. You made mistakes because you didn't listen to advice and because life is about experience. You learned the rules of the road and gained valuable experience, because you practiced and worked at it. You worked at this because you needed to; you realized you needed this skill—it is a necessity. Marriage is much like learning to drive. Even with the feelings, desire, and intention to love, communicate, and forgive, we may not have had good role models, instruction, or counsel. Maybe we disregarded God's Word or didn't even know of God's plan for us. You had all the hope, enthusiasm, the willpower and a wish to make it work. Slowly, you may have realized that marriage is tough and, instead of working on it or knowing how to work on it, you became disillusioned, frustrated, or complacent. Or, maybe you did work on it— read a book, listened to others, changed certain behaviors— without lasting success. Maybe, you have given your marriage your "all" to no avail. Now, you want to give up or shut down.

I encourage you to be bold and brave! In Christ, you CAN move from the darkness of hurts and live in the Light of Christ.

Surrendering to the Lord and reading God's Word with the Holy Spirit in you guiding you, you absolutely will behold a wondrous revolution in your lives together. If you are already blessed with a good marriage, consider this a tune-up, building upon the hard work and commitment that you have already realized in a good relationship. You and your spouse are worth this much.

What spawned this endeavor?

In the 1970's, Edith Schaeffer—and others—occasionally did marriage retreats. I was fortunate enough be at a few as a kid; later, I was able to rediscover her notes. Upon finding the notes, I combined them with my own knowledge gained while researching and ghostwriting a book for an eminent Christian psychologist and used this knowledge for sermons and also in Bible studies for couples. In my research, I noticed that critical biblical insights were overlooked. This frustrated me. I felt frustrated that so many books on marriage are written for the Christian world based on man's psychological theories while God's Word is barely addressed or treated as a buffet that one might just pick and choose the easiest or most attractive bits. Even worse, some materials even take God's Word and take the Word out of context, twisting it to serve the author's purpose while not glorifying Christ and His "true Truths." The main points God has for us are missing. This book is the fruit of the combined work and is designed to be used as a tool for a retreat, seminar, pastoral counseling, professional Christian counseling, sermon guide, and/or personal devotion and for me, a how-to-guide that I can keep going back to for advice and help.

How was this book made?

This book is not about *my* theories or some personal agenda; rather, this work is based on God's precepts on building a great marriage. My role in this is reading the Bible, conducting research, extracting prime precepts, practicing them, observing the results, and laying them out for you. While I understand the concepts are easy and the practice can be difficult, this is completely doable even in the most barren circumstances.

This love and marriage book is also based on over 25 years of careful exegetical research and pastoral counseling experience. Primarily, this series is based carefully on the Bible's timeless truths. It is not about psychological fads or theories. The goal is to find the best real answers from the timeless truths for real help to those who just need to know or who are down and out and do not know where to go. The main viewpoints and directions are what the Lord gives us from His Word so that we can better prepare and practice for the second most important thing we will ever do in life (the first being our salvation).

In addition to the Word, research, and experience, over 100 couples in fulfilling, long-lasting marriages were interviewed (this facilitated the "Tips"). To round this out, some key research was gleaned from the Schaeffer Institute, the Fuller Institute, and Fuller Seminary. Included in interviews and consultations were: Ray Stedman, Chuck Miller, Dr. John Gottman, Edith Schaeffer, Dr. Julie Gorman, Dr. Archibald Heart, John Stott, Dr. Clyde Narramore and many other professionals including many seasoned pastors and Christian counselors.

This is a work is also one of practice—the trials and errors of a married man who has made the mistakes and tried his best to be better, who has failed and has succeeded to be the best spouse that one can be. I have never been unfaithful, praise God; but, I have had to examine how faithful I have been in my loving and adoration, in my cherishing, forgiving, affections, even when times have been bad and daunting. I am a work in progress, as we all are.

You have in your hands a colossal endeavor that has been simplified and made practical for you.

You CAN build a healthy marriage that glorifies Christ as Lord.

Who is this book for?

It is for me. It is for you. This book is for couples seeking pre-marriage counseling and for married couples who desire God's call in their marriage or refreshment of the marital relationship. It is also for those who are having doubts, troubles, or hurts. It is for those who are feeling overwhelmed and, maybe, hopeless in their relationship. This is for those who just want to grow closer to the Lord and live in a marriage that is blessed and led by Christ. This is for those who want a "how to," an easy-to-read, comprehensive book on marriage that has all they need, and that they can keep referring to. This is an invitation to come see what our Lord, through His Word, has to say about building a great, lasting marriage.

How to use this marriage book

You use this book easily—just read it and be in prayer. Ask, *How can I change and apply these precepts and be humble to make it work?* You can discuss this with your spouse and/or in a small group. This book has a 'tag-team' approach. I will present a biblical description, such as an aspect of Love— what it is, how to know it, and apply it into your life and marriage. Next, I will present a key aspect on how to build an effectual marriage. In addition, we have discussion questions to challenge, inspire, provoke and help you process these true Truth from Scripture and the ideas distilled from those passages. Then, we have dozens of "Marriage Tips," that will help you focus in the right direction, give practical help, and encouragement. You might consider reading and practicing one tip each day. (See the Appendix I for a complete listing.)

How to use this marriage book as a workshop

In addition to using this personally in your marriage and in fellowship in small groups, you could also use this in a workshop setting. This endeavor will be in a seminar and or a devotional format. I suggest that you have people read the book first, or one chapter at a time, and discuss the key points of need followed by the questions. You might go over one chapter for a day for a seminar or three chapters for a weekend retreat. Any chapter(s) can be used; however, the main ones I suggest are, Chapter 3 *Building a Wondrous Marriage*, Chapter 6 *Marriage where Real Love is Practiced,* Chapter 7 *Cherish and Respect*, and you can have a seminar with a financial planner and do Chapter 18 *Marriage Money Matters* with the Appendix III on Budgeting ideas, or a seminar with Chapter 19 *Divorce Proof Your Marriage* or, Chapter 20 *The Marriage Tune-up!*

The passages, main points, and some applications are given; you can read, be challenged, equipped, inspired and encouraged to make a wondrous marriage begin! In addition, I will take you into a journey of what love is and what it is not. You will get an aspect of love and a session on what a biblical marriage looks like to work on at your own pace.

This book can be used as a personal guide for individuals and can be done individually; ideally, you would do this alongside your spouse or fiancé, small group, or with a qualified pastor or counselor. This book can also be used for a community workshop or class.

I recommend that this be a journey to be done together as a couple, and you can share with a counselor or a small group or marriage retreat. The appendixes are additional resources for you and for counselors. It is best to follow a sequence that looks like this: Read the passages and curriculum, discuss with your spouse, be committed to listen, be open for criticism, be forgiving and remember the Fruit of the Spirit from Galatians, Chapter Five. Try to practice the 'Tips" as much as possible. Then, follow through with a counselor or mentor, and remember to stay in prayer with an attitude of *I can do this, I can have a wondrous marriage, I can make it work.*

Let us look at how to prepare and build for a successful marriage.

First, read 1 Corinthians 7:1-11, 39-40, 13:1-13, be committed to learn, forgive and engage God's Truth and apply His precepts to your life. The revolution for the healthier marriage begins.

Nevertheless, God's solid foundation stands firm, sealed with this inscription: "The Lord knows those who are his," and, "Everyone who confesses the name of the Lord must turn away from wickedness." 2 Timothy 2:19

(Please note this book is not for the person in an abusive relationship. If there is abuse of any sort, seek qualified professional help right away. If you are in danger, please get out and get help immediately and contact law enforcement.)

PROLOGUE

A Look at Love

If I speak in the tongues of men or of angels, but do not have love, I am only a resounding gong or a clanging cymbal. If I have the gift of prophecy and can fathom all mysteries and all knowledge, and if I have a faith that can move mountains, but do not have love, I am nothing. 1 Corinthians 13:1-2

We are going to look at the aspects of love from the classic and most effectual definition ever devised or conceived—the one given to us by God Himself, 1 Corinthians 13. I encourage you to read and reread this passage many times, as many times as possible.

Key marriage tip: Remember real love is sacrificial. Our call as Christians is to go further than what our expectations, pride, hurt, or the world expects.

Be in prayer, be honest and self-examining, and see how you can challenge yourself and grow in the knowledge and fruit of real effectual love.

Be in prayer to be a person who loves and receive love truly for this is how the Lord loves you. Know it, feel it, and live it.

If you want a great marriage, you have to know what love is and what love is not; you have to give love and receive it. In so doing, you will be able to cherish and respect one another. By working in Scripture and seeking Christ, you will have a deeper relationship with Christ to apply love and practice forgiveness—real love—which will help you to thrive in relationships. Effectual love is paramount in building a successful marriage that honors God; such a relationship has the power to shape, mold, and lead your family and others around you.

Do you want to know what love is?

To find out, carefully read the 1 Corinthians 13 passage and see it as a character depiction of Jesus Christ Himself, Lord and Savior. In fact, as you read this passage, you can even find and replace the key word of love with the Name of Jesus, as the NIV passage states, like Jesus is patient, Jesus is kind, etc. Let's see how this works:

Love is patient means that Jesus is patient as He works in and through you!

What would this love of patience do for you and your marriage?

Love is kind means that Jesus is kind and cares for you, even when you do not deserve it!

What would this love of kindness do for you and your marriage?

Love is not easily angered means that Jesus is not touchy or resentful or out to get you. He wants to help you!

What would this love of controlling your anger do for you and your marriage?

Love keeps no record of wrongs means that Jesus forgives you when we seek it from Him!

What would this love of no score keeping do for you and your marriage?

Love protects means that Jesus is protecting as He has staying power in and through you!

What would this love of protection do for you and your marriage?

Love hopes means that Jesus is enduring and points you to the future!

What would this love of optimism do for you and your marriage?

Love is perseveres means that Jesus refuses to quit or give up on you!

What would this love of perseverance do for you and your marriage?

Love never fails means that Jesus love for you will last forever!

What would this love of not giving up do for you and your marriage?

Love never quits means Jesus never quits. He does not give up on you!

What would this love of never giving up do for you and your marriage?

After you see our Lord in this passage. Now try to see yourself; insert your name into it like this—Joe is patient, Joanne is kind, and so forth. You will see what we have to work on.

Therefore, my dear friends, as you have always obeyed—not only in my presence, but now much more in my absence—continue to work out your salvation with fear and trembling, for it is God who works in you to will and to act in order to fulfill his good purpose. Philippians 2:12-13

CHAPTER 1

Have a Better Image of Marriage

Therefore, my brothers and sisters, make every effort to confirm your calling and election. For if you do these things, you will never stumble, and you will receive a rich welcome into the eternal kingdom of our Lord and Savior Jesus Christ. 1 Peter 1:10-11

You can have better!

The marriage God has for you may not be the one you are in right now! No, I am not talking about leaving; I am talking about cleaving. What He has is greater than your vision, your past, your hurts, what you have right now, or even what you think you want.

What our Lord has for you and your family is greater than you can imagine. We need to understand this and build upon it! God wants His righteousness, love and Fruit poured out onto you. In turn, this love of God will flow from you onto your loved ones and others around you. He wants His children to get Him and get what this journey of life is all about. He wants us to know Him and build upon what He gives, to live out lives of love, fruit and faith. We can do this by His Word, as beings made by Christ, received by Christ in our faith and fruit, hope by our trust and by our obedience in Him. Our Christian life and marriage will be more triumphant!

Key marriage tip: A successful Christian marriage that lasts is between two imperfect people in Christ, who refuse to give up on each other just as Christ never gives up on us.

You can have a better relationship!

The weddings in the Bible—the ones Jesus attended—are Jewish; the weddings are communal and relational. We often forget this. This is where the marriage is consummated and celebrated with family and friends. This community proves that you are not in this alone. This is also a promise of deliverance and reward for being faithful as Christ takes the Church as His Bride, and the dowry, which He paid on the cross.

You can have better intimacy!

The wedding feast is also an expression of God's intimacy and agency with us. In Revelation, it is also a contrast between the horror of evil and the joys of goodness. A Christ-centered, God-glorifying marriage is compared with our salvation as to a banquet—a most high privilege and honor in the ancient world. In Him, we are cleansed, saved, and redeemed. We belong to Him; as such, our church, our home, our lives must be sanctified unto Him.

(Isaiah 25:6-9; Matthew 22:1-22, 26-29; 2 Corinthians 11:2-3; Ephesians 5:26; Colossians 1:22; 1 Thessalonians 5:15-24; 1 Timothy 4:16; 1 John 3:3; Revelation 7:17; 19:1-10)

How can I have better? Having a better marriage is a matter of focus, effort, and a willingness to know a better image of what God has for our marriage. We must be able and willing to engage it wholeheartedly as an act of worship. Accordingly, Jewish and Christian marriages are acts of worship—an essential component of communion and community. We communicate our love, adoration, and gratitude to Christ, together as a church locally, as a Church universally, and with all of creation "in concert." When we realize we worship Christ as Lord first and foremost, we have better!

How can we do this? We must begin by seeing our marriages as an act of worship. How you view and treat God? How you honor and give Him praise is manifested in our relationships, especially that with our spouse. Your worship of Christ as Lord, will impact who and how you are in your home and family. To have better, we must honor Christ in our words and deeds, and pursue them with passion.

How do I make this work? We must not seek our fulfillment in being married, but in being fulfilled in Christ, who loves us so much that we are able to fully love in our marriages. Our joy is to come from our relationship in Christ, not from our spouses. Marriage was not designed to complete a person. Our completion can only be found in Our Lord and Savior—our One Foundation. Marriage is the place that we share the joy, love, and passion of full intimacy. Christ is the Foundation, and marriage is the structure in which we build our relationship with our spouses, children, and selves to, with, and in Christ and each other. Happiness and joy are byproducts that may or may not always happen. Marriage is not about being happy and fulfilled. Marriage is absolutely about glorifying God. We can strive to be better and make our marriages better. Happiness and contentment may come, too.

What else can I do? It's necessary to see your marriage as a stewardship—you are to be a good steward, a proper manager, to be your best for His glory, your spouse and family. Why? They are created in the image of God, just as you are. Your spouse is a child of God just as you are. And God deeply loves your spouse just as Christ loves you. He wants you treated with dignity, respect, just as he wants you to treat your spouse.

We are called to exalt Christ as Lord; He also calls us to exalt your spouse as His child as you become one in Him.

Consider this. If you are unfaithful in your marriage (not just in sexual sin) by not doing your duty to love, adore, cherish, encourage and respect your spouse, you are not properly worshiping Christ as Lord. Rather, we become consumed with our hurts or passions or expectations. We cannot see Jesus or what He has for your family that is far better that what you have now or could have on your own.

Let God use your marriage to help build your faith as an edifying tool that builds and encourages and points to His Glory.

What if the misery never goes away?

Then I heard what sounded like a great multitude, like the roar of rushing waters and like loud peals of thunder, shouting: "Hallelujah! For our Lord God Almighty reigns". Revelation 19:6

We can have motivation. We have staying power by staying our trust in Christ. Know this: God is the One who vindicates. He will make all things right. If you are in a an abusive relationship, get out now and put your faith in the Lord. For you who are seeking to turn around a dysfunctional (not abusive) relationship, understand that God will heal you when you build in Him. When you rest and trust in Christ, you and your spouse allow Christ to lead you so that you may cleave and be one in Him.

Key marriage tip: The number one reason Christian marriages survive and succeed is a mutual respect for one another and a surrender to the Lordship of Christ.

One of the great hopes of the Christian is one day we will hear, see, feel and profoundly experience the shouts of praise and thanksgiving, all coming from Heaven, in the very Temple of God. All will fall prostrate before God as we sing His praise. *Hallelujah, let us be glad and rejoice in Him!* All will know that salvation is from God and His power, judgments, and purposes are just and pure. All will know He is a God who is real and trustworthy, who carries out His promises and His holy plan. Until then, we live for Him, and put into ourselves in His call and precepts.

Be more diligent!

All that we are and can be in our lives and marriages result from Christ's sacrifice of redemption, His permanence, and His love for us. He lived, died, and rose again for you and me and for our spouses, too! All we are to do is trust and obey Him, and as we continue in this endeavor, He gives us even more empowerment for enduring life and performing ministry along with His special favor and peace! Even if we do not see Jesus, He sees us, loves us, and helps us persevere. This may seem unattainable or even unfathomable in our hurts and anger when we are under stress or the hostile occupations of life. However, we can do this because we have access to His empowerment; we are literally kept by God through faith.

Your marriage is a journey. It is to be grown and cultivated just like our faith.

As we grow in our faith, we become even more precious to God and He will preserve us through the trials of marriage and life. This is one of the reasons we are called to grow in Him! When we receive faith and salvation that we do not deserve or earn, we consequently respond with gratitude for what He has given; we have more compassion, staying power, and capacity for our spouses, and we will even desire more. To do this, we need Christ's empowerment. We must look to Christ and not to our hurts. This will come from knowing Him, growing in Him, and having the desire for more.

Marriage and the family is the prime place we Christian men and women exercise our faith.

We have to be reminded of our focus—Christ—to persevere. We have to guard against hurts, causing our shortsightedness. We must choose not to be myopic. If we choose to focus on the distress, this is a failure on our part to either utilize His call or seek to understand and apply His precepts to life and home (Isaiah 42:19; John 9:39-41; 2 Corinthians 4:4).

Marriage and the family is the prime place we Christian men and women exercise our *calling*.

In Judaism, this referred to being close to God. In the calling, we know what to do and be. We do not call on Jesus for our salvation because we receive it only as an act of undeserving grace that we cannot get on our own by merit or birthright. This extraordinary gift of Grace leads us to gratitude. From that gratitude, we are to exercise grace in our home. Especially since we are transformed, we are called to show it and grow in it. Our further hope in this is that the Holy Spirit gives us testimony and empowers our's; we are then to persevere in our faith. This is an aspect of our assurance of salvation; what we have done with what He has given is the evidence of who we are in Christ. We must practice what God gives, as God gives us salvation and eternal life that we continue in the applications of our faith into the lives of our spouses.

(Matthew 10:22; 24:12-13; Romans 12; Galatians 4:6; Ephesians 1:4-6; 5:6, 22-23; Philippians 2:12-13; 2 Timothy 2:19; Hebrews 3:6; 1 John 3:10-14)

A Christian marriage is not passive. One cannot just sit and do nothing. One cannot put the least amount of effort into anything and expect to get something wonderful. Weariness and frustration can occur, though; for the Christian, remember to lay your burdens at the feet of the Lord and invite Him to work through you and in you so that you may persevere in Him in the vows that you made to your spouse.

It is a call to press on, to persevere, to continue, to be diligent, so that we practice and grow our faith and produce fruit, character, and virtue. Please do not be shortsighted in matters of your faith and the opportunities Christ has and will still bring. If we do not have a desire to pursue the will of God, we have to ask ourselves *why* and *what is in the way*. Most, if not all of the time, it is the desire of sin that blocks us. Sometimes we may not recognize sin; we may rationalize it away. This happens especially when sin is "dumbed down" or **minimized** and shown as OK in the media and entertainment. (The media and entertainment surround us, and some of it is ok—just remember to guard what is good.) Our election is proven by our obedience and growth in Christ!

Remember, Christ is our living Hope that will never fade away!

We are chosen by God and by God alone! The Holy Spirit sets us apart. We are able to hear and receive His Words of grace and life. We need to be reminded of what we have and who we are in Christ. If we do not remember or if we put away the Truth, we will soon forget and replace His guidance either with our frailty or with the ways of the world.

This hope gives us the staying power to be better in our Christian lives and relationships and the world we live in. The goal: To be Christ-sighted, not shortsighted. Do not lose your motivation in Christ; see yourselves as complete in Him.

Be reminded, you can do it!

For that one day, the time of sorrow is over; now is the wedding feast of the Lamb that we as the faithful can partake in as God rewards us for our good deeds and faithfulness. Then we hear, *blessed are those who are invited to the wedding feast of the Lamb.* These words come from God! If you think you can't do this, then pray; in fact, do what John did in the passage—fall down prostrate before God in fear and awe of His majesty and presence (Revelation 19:1-10).

How to I keep centered on Christ? See your life as He wants to see it, as an expression of honor, glory, and gratitude to God for who He is and what He has done. It expresses our praise and honor for His glory. In Christ, we are like a bride married to a groom, as Israel was a bride of God. This is a celebration of our salvation in Him (Matthew 5:12; Revelation 21:2).

Key marriage tip: The number one reason why marriages fail is because of the breakdown in communication. To succeed in marriage and in life is to listen and be willing and open to the understanding of your spouse and others.

Our authentic vindication is that we have received our justification in Christ. It is sealed and more valuable that we will ever know. Evil has no vindication and will have no acquittal. When we are faithful, no matter what we have experienced or been through, He is with us, and He, Jesus Himself, will give us vindication. Then, the question we are to seek is *How then do I live my Christian life? Do I live as a response to whom He is and what He has done, or rather, as I see fit?* In context, this is also about bringing the Truth of Christ to our churches and using churches to bring His Truth to the world. Thus, the church must remain in Him and see His Supremacy; churches of any Christian denomination should not allow us to further human ideas or agendas contrary to His

Word and call. This also means we are not to allow ourselves to bow to complacency, idolatry, social and cultural changes, social "correctness" or "tolerance", or apostasy!

Key marriage tip: When a successful marriage lasts between two imperfect people, it is because they refuse to give up on the work of the Lord.

The marriage passages in Matthew 22 and in Revelation 19 are about a proclamation not just to know and trust God, but to praise Him with a heart that anticipates His goodness and realizes His faithfulness, because we are already victorious in Christ. This *marriage* supper is about our faith in, relationship with, and commitment to Christ; it is our response to Him from our gratitude and declaration to one another, His Church, to be prepared in knowledge and faith in Him, and to live our lives worthy for Him. Thus, this passage is also about discipleship; we learn of Him so to be in Him, and live worthy with our redemption that we have received (Ephesians 5:25-27).

But Christ is faithful as the Son over God's house. And we are his house, if indeed we hold firmly to our confidence and the hope in which we glory. Hebrews 3:6

Questions to challenge, inspire, and equip you to be better in your commitment, love, and marriage:

Read Matthew 22:1-22; Ephesians 5:25-27

1. What are you grateful to God for? What happens when Christians forget to be grateful? How does ingratitude affect the church and call that Christ gives us?

2. What can motivate you more to serve Christ wholeheartedly and righteously? How about together?

3. How can the fact that Christ is all supreme, all powerful and strong, all mighty, and the ruler of all things help you move from leading by personal agendas to leading with His precepts, character, Fruit, and call?

4. In Christ we have immeasurable intimacy and community with God as His child. How can that motivate you to live with your eyes more on Him and less on your fears or circumstances? How can this affect your marriage?

5. Do you know that your justification in Christ is sealed and more valuable than you will ever know? How does this affect your righteousness and purity? How will this build your marriage?

CHAPTER 2

What About My Heart?

The heart is deceitful above all things and beyond cure.
Who can understand it? Jeremiah 17:9

Leading your heart—not letting your heart lead you!

The world tells us that being *in* love virtually guarantees a perfect marriage; this idea encourages us to follow our hearts. Is this true? Does this work? Is it biblical? Are we ready to really follow our hearts? Does the heart's desire equal what is best? Is there something we can do to help our heart be content and not be led into what is false or dysfunctional?

The World's Theme is Fake and Fickle

The world (that includes us) beckons us to "follow our hearts," as it is reflected in entertainment, poems, TV, movies, fairy tales, and romance novels. We may even hear this from our families and friends. Don't misunderstand me. There is certainly some truth and wisdom in this guidance. However, there is also a big problem. The heart is emotion-driven and based on feelings, desires, and—sometimes—circumstance. In this, there is much room for sin. Hearing that the heart is sinful is not politically correct in the secular world, nor is it popular in the evangelical Christian world, but it is true and biblically True. The heart is evil! We need to understand this and remember it. The Bible is clear on this, and this is God's Truth. Why is the heart considered evil? It seeks what is not always best and wants what it can't have. It longs for a person or thing to smooth and soothe it, but what it usually desires only brings about hopelessness, dysfunction, and strife. Unless we completely guard our hearts with the truth, wisdom, discernment, and love of Christ, we will sin with our hearts.

God does not just urge us to love; He commands us to!

What is more important and effectual? God commands us to love! As a good and perfect Father, He gives us the meaning of true love, He gives us direction, and He gives Himself as the example. So, look over these questions, first between God and yourself. After you have answered the questions, put on your listening ears and ask your spouse to read and answer them, also. Let your spouse know that you will do your very best to really pay attention and attend to his/her answers and concerns.

- How is your marriage?
- Is it working for you?
- Are you working for it?
- What if your marriage is not going according to plan?
- What if you feel that you and your spouse are drifting apart or are already distant or feeling hopeless?
- What if you feel you have tried with all of your might, yet you are still frustrated or overwhelmed?
- Is there something we can do to repair and extend our marriages to be better than they were before—even on their best days?

From what I have seen from research and experienced in doing marriage counseling, we are in trouble. Our families are being torn apart as if we were in a war, and each one of us was a faction, reeling in our hurt and expelling out our anger. Many people are very unhappy and disillusioned, living a pathetic life instead of a triumphant life because they are miserable in their marriages. People in my church and even people in my family are in this trouble—perhaps in your's, too. Why the strife and turmoil? In truth, it is because they follow a conflicting, sinful heart that seeks desires over Christ.

The dating and courtship is over; you are married now. You need to find a way to live in it, make it work, and thrive with joy. Even if you feel that you have made wrong choices, God can use you to work it out for the best. You can have a "love dare" that will allow you to rebuild, rehabilitate, and improve—take what God has given and use His tools for relationship bliss! This challenge also assumes you are not in an abusive relationship and that both people are mentally and physically healthy and able to relate. If this is not you, please seek professional help from a licensed Christian counselor or pastor before undertaking this challenge.

Key marriage tip: We must allow Christ to be the leader of our heart and our marriage!

The Bible tells us, *He who trusts in himself* (meaning following one's own heart) *is a fool, but he who walks in wisdom is kept safe.* Proverbs 28:26

What about my heart? Because our hearts are corrupted with sin and can lead us to what is false, actions based on the heart alone can result in indecision, unpredictability, inconsistency, shallow, and ever-changing desires that lead us in multiple wrong directions and blind us to what is better and more fulfilling. So, how will we be led in the right direction (Psalm 37:4; Proverbs 23:7; 27:19; Matthew 15:19)?

Key marriage tip: Remember the health of our marriage will not only 'affect' (influence) you and your spouse, but also has 'effect' (result) on your children, family, extended family, church, friends, acquaintances and the reputation of our Lord. What you do and say does matter, and it is watched!

A Heart for Marriage

A mature Christian heart is focused, formed, and straightened in and from our growth in Christ. It is a heart of conviction in Christ, overflowing with gratitude for Who and What He has done, with vigor, power and authority to lead others to Christ. This heart is a focus to look upon Christ as the foundation of our marriage to be better and to hear His call to edify and love the people in our family, especially our spouse.

We lead our heart by taking our lead from our Lord, and we can then lead our marriage in confidence that the love we will learn and practice is first given to us by Christ. This is especially important for the husband, to lead—not out of coercion or conceit—out of a heart that truly loves. This lead will be followed by one who will give respect—the wife. Our fire is from the precepts of Scripture and the leading of the Holy Spirit. We lead by example and sincerity with a kind heart protecting our people, by a gentle spirit, always in integrity and all in the Fruit of the Spirit (2 Corinthians 6:11-7:16; Colossians 3:18-4:1).

The enemy of our hearts is the pride that is built upon our hurts and disappointments; this creates bad thoughts and attitudes. We must be aware that bad thoughts and actions lead to bad lives. In marriage, when we lose our way, we cause derailment to the contentment of our home; and if it continues, this becomes a train wreck for all who are in our family and around us. This is why Christ calls us to purposefully focus ourselves on Christ, His precepts, and His presence. When we focus on Christ, our attention is off other things and distractions—even sin! *Things above* are heavenly matters; *things below/on earth* are our desires, agendas, and sin. Our heart and marriage are led better to His direction and purpose (Matthew 6:33; Romans 8:5; Philippians 1:23; 4:8; 1 John 2:15-17).

Guard the Enemy of the Heart

As Christians, we need to <u>always</u> be seeking maturity; we must protect and guard the hearts of ourselves and others in our family and care from distractions and corruptions! This is why Christ tells us to *set your minds,* meaning to place Christ first and foremost. If you are wondering *Why*, consider what you are doing. Why are you married? If the purpose is for selfish reasons only or anything other than the growth of your family, then get help and get in the Word. Your heart has to be pointed in the right direction in order to be led in the right direction!

We must be aware that our hurts, pride, and bad thoughts will lead to bad actions and bad lives. In marriage, when we lose our way, we cause pain to so many others—family, friends, coworkers, acquaintances, and others—who watch, so our derailment becomes a train wreck for all who are behind us. This is why Christ's precepts and His presence for the entirety of our lives matters, because it matters to us and others around us. When we focus on Christ, our attention is off other things, like our disappointments and pride and distractions—even sin! Heavenly values will translate into earthy values that will translate into a joyful marriage that others can see and emulate when we are centered on Christ, allowing His work in and through us to lead others better to His direction and purpose (Matthew 6:33; Romans 8:5; Philippians 1:23; 4:8; 1 John 2:15-17).

Key marriage tip: A wondrous marriage does not just happen. You have to work it. You must push forward, and move away from pride and into the Fruit of the Spirit. Cultivate communication and listening to each other. You will have set backs, so always play it forward, play it hard and push in love.

A Great Marriage is built upon Love, the Spiritual Fruit

Therefore, as God's chosen people, holy and dearly loved, clothe yourselves with compassion, kindness, humility, gentleness and patience. Bear with each other and forgive whatever grievances you may have against one another. Forgive as the Lord forgave you. And over all these virtues put on love, which binds them all together in perfect unity. Colossians 3:12-14

Love is the spiritual fruit that is built from real, godly character and our commitment to Christ. It is the fiber of our moral center that stretches throughout our being, embracing and holding together our relationships when it is sealed as a choice and commitment, not just a matter of feelings or desires. Love will synergistically combine with the other characteristics of our Lord that flow from the Fruit of the Spirit. This fruit will promote our ability to relate and grow in our marriages (and our other relationships) to better others, as well as ourselves (Galatians 5:22-23).

Love begins—real love, that is—when you have a firm grasp on what the simple yet profound message of 1 Corinthians 13.

It happens when the presumptions and games are out of the way, when open communication is happening, and when both of you are growing in the faith. If you are willing to work on it, and there is no abuse going on, the love that was once felt will rise again. If we focus on Christ and not on our hurts, we will care enough to listen, put in the efforts for one another, and love will come. Love cannot be forced, manipulated, conjured up, or pretended into reality.

Key marriage tip: You cannot trust your heart; you can only trust the Lord!

You can try to force love for a while, but it would be like teaching a dog to walk on its two hind legs. It will be able to do it for a little while, but not very long, and not very well! You have to let Love happen as stipulated in 1 Corinthians

13. But, this love is above all patient, so allow yourselves to be patient while love builds. Remember, you are married. Be committed and love will start to work.

Key marriage tip: Remember, you can't change your spouse. You can only change yourself. The work begins in you first—without your seeking control of another. The work begins with you learning how to truly love and loving another.

Questions to challenge, inspire, and equip you to be better in your commitment, love, and marriage:

Read Psalm 37:4; Proverbs 23:7; 27:19; 28:26; Jeremiah 17:9 ; Matthew 15:19; John 17:25-26

1. What do you think it means to follow your heart? How have you done this? What happened? What causes this to fail?
2. What and how do you think will help you lead your marriage in the right direction? What can you do to not seek to control your spouse, but rather trust in Christ?
3. At this point, what do you think you need to do to find a way to live in your marriage (assuming there is no abuse going on), make it work, even thrive with joy?
4. At this point, what do you think you need to do to rebuild, rehab, and improve your marriage?
5. Can you make a commitment to take what God has given and use His tools for relationship bliss?

Spend time in prayer and commit to pray for your spouse when you first wake up, when you go to bed, and throughout the day!

CHAPTER 3

Building a Wondrous Marriage

A new command I give you: Love one another. As I have loved you, so you must love one another. By this all men will know that you are my disciples, if you love one another. John 13:34-35

God's Theme is Genuine and Stable

This passage in John 13 should be known to you and me, but its practice may be new, difficult, or unpracticed. This is the Love Challenge The distinguishing characteristic of Christ's followers is that we are deeply and eternally loved. We are created in love, saved by love and called to know and exercise love. The application of this is that our standard of love must be Christ's love for us (John 3:16, 14-15).

The call to *Love one another* applies first and foremost to your spouse.

This means sacrificial, unselfish, determined love; the change Jesus makes in John 13 is from "neighbor" to "one another" to make sure the theme is community. Our change is from seeing our spouse as the opponent to the partner, from the problem to the focus of our love. Love confirms the genuineness of Jesus and us as followers! This is also a template on the importance and value of friendships and building an effective church!

(Mark 12:30-31; Luke 10:27; John 13:34-35; 15:12, 17; Romans 12:10; 13:8; 14:13; 1 Thessalonians 3:12; 4:9; 2 Thessalonians 1:3; 1 Peter 1:22; 1 John 3:11, 3:22; 4:8; 23; 4:7, 11-12; 2 John 1: 5)

Key marriage tip: The Christian life is meant as a journey to live with the goal of leaving behind a legacy of real love. This life of our's was never meant to be lived in the darkness of selfishness and pride.

The prime purpose of marriage is to grow us closer to the love and the Person of Christ and His Likeness.

The call to *Love one another* is *Agape*, which means "self giving" and "sacrificial". Agape love is more concerned with others than self. We are to be more concerned with our spouse than ourselves. We must remember that spouses were never intended to "complete" us. Spouses—marriage—were created so that we would have a partnership, companionship, a living example of the love of Jesus Christ, a living example of a covenant before God. Spouses should not or be expected to complete us, and they cannot. Our completion is in Jesus Christ alone.

Agape love was used in Classic Greek literature to refer to someone who was generously favored by a god. (For instance, if Zeus liked you, he would bestow great things.) It conveys the idea of a person giving all his or her love, or favor, to someone else rather than to self. It is a love that is not earned; in contrast, agape love is relational and given freely. It also refers to parents giving all of their love for their child. This is the love we are called to receive and give out, to know and to put into practice, to experience and help others experience, too!

God chooses His Words carefully. In the New Testament, *agape* love was used to make a similar point, as God gives to each of us all of His love. It is a love that is bestowed without expectations of a response from the other. We should give it to our spouse even when they do not return it. *Agape* love is the greatest example of real and true love, as this is what our Lord Jesus Christ did when He died for our sins.

Consequently, God's *agape* love gave us His forbearance and rescue from the punishment that we deserved. Rather than receiving what we should have, we received His favor without earning it. This is the prime evangelism and relationship building tool. As the John passage continues to say, *All men will know that you are my disciples.* When we *love one another*, we prove and exhibit Christ! We build our spouse, we build our family and we build our church. This is our "mark", the prime characteristic that makes us friendly and connected to the one we married and even to others, and how we are to be known—by what Christ does with us and calls us to. We are to love one another—period! We are to love our husbands; we are to love our wives with no strings attached! This is the mold for the form that we use to display God's love to the world (John 13:34-35; 15:13-17; Galatians 5:22; 1 John 2:10; 3:14-16)!

Key marriage tip: Do not let your pride and hurt control you; rather, allow Christ' love to motivate you!

Love confirms the authenticity of Jesus!

* *How much God so loves you!*
* How much God has so loves you!
* How much He so loves your spouse!
* How much He so loves your marriage!
* How much He so loves your family!

When you are loved much, you will love much and then you will do much, so much more—in your life and in the lives of others!

Love confirms the authenticity of Jesus' followers!

Who God is and what He is like have been and continue to be resounding questions for the ages of humanity. Philosophers and theologians have pondered this question since the beginning. We can know for sure who He is, what He is like, and how He expresses Himself to us. God's love is who He is. His Love confirms the authenticity of us as His followers, because it is an attribute He calls us to emulate. Our primary objective for this emulation is the one whom we married!

As my mother and stepfather were fighting with each other, Francis Schaeffer offered them this adage: "It is natural to love those who love us, but it is supernatural to love those who hate us." He told this story that still, thirty years later, resounds in me. It is a true story that happened during World War II. Hitler issued a friendly request in the late '30s that all Christian groups were to cooperate and communicate together. By 1940, it became a formal command that all religious groups (meaning all Christian denominations even though Lutheran was dominant in Germany), must unite and cooperate. This sounds good on the outside, but it was done so that he could control them. Half complied and half refused. Those who complied with the order did not have their properties seized or the people themselves "disappeared," while those who did not comply faced these ruthless persecutions. In every church that resisted, many people died in concentration camps and families were torn apart.

When Hitler was dead and the Allies liberated Germany, feelings of deep bitterness seeped in and ran deep between these churches factions, both those who were complacent and those who resisted. Families were still being torn apart after the war was over because of the tensions and strife that were brought into each home. Something had to be done as the American-occupying Army and its chaplains and soldiers had to intervene on many occasions.

They finally decided that the circumstances did not honor God or the mission of the Church and caused irreparable harm to many families whose loyalties were divided between these two church factions. They realized they needed healing and somehow to forgive; but how? How could this tremendous hurt be cured? So, leaders of each faction convened for a retreat to pray. For a week, each person spent time in prayer, examining Christ's commands, confronting their own hearts in the light of Scripture and seeking guidance from the Holy Spirit. A miracle occurred; they forgave one another and came back together in real, cooperative unity.

My uncle asked my parents, *What did you learn from this?* My stepfather made a cynical remark and my mom ran into the other room. Later, at a quiet and awkward dinner, he said, *"These people faced more hurt and toil than any marriage could ever face today. As they sought God and confessed their resentment and bitterness to one another, they were able to yield to His control and heal their churches and families. This is the same with you; the Holy Spirit can fashion a spirit of unity amongst you too. Love must fill your hearts and dissolve your hatred; you must lead your heart to love and not let your heart lead you away."* (Francis Schaeffer, cir 1978)

Key marriage tip: See and practice your marriage as an offering to our Lord. To be poured out to Him so it affects all of our relationships. The learning and exercising of your faith will be the prime way of building your relationship and cherishing and respecting your spouse, even in difficult situations.

Always be respectful and loving, and allow the character and Fruit of the Spirit to flow through you, being respectful and courteous to your spouse, even when they are not to you. In time, you will see a change. If you are not naturally courteous and respectful, seek a mentor or professional help. Allow the Lord to work on you!

The challenge of this authentic love is that life and marriage is complicated and difficult and people, as in your spouse, will always disappoint us. We will always be disappointing back, and to others around us. But, God's enduring love will never disappoint us, because God does not retaliate back to us when we deserve it. Therefore, when we endure by and with love, we can be restrained and not retaliate when life and people are difficult. Keep in mind that Jesus gives as much time and patience as possible, because He wants us to live a life that bears His fruit. When we do, our lives will be marked with endurance and patience.

Here are two essential attitudes to have if you are serious about following God's precepts in marriage:

First, have an attitude of Fellowship: Fellowship (*Koinonia*) is the Christian catchphrase for getting together. Perhaps it is overused and underused. We overuse it to describe anything from hanging out to having Communion; we under use it by not taking the reality of practice and the depth of its meaning to heart! Biblical fellowship is a partnership of relationships and resources that contains good communication, cooperation, and mutual benefit. The powerful Holy Spirit is our true partner in the Church and in our marriage. This is true because of what Christ has done for us. Now consider how you can be better to have fellowship with your spouse, this will be the fun factor in your marriage!

Second, have an attitude of real Intimacy: The Church has taught for centuries that sex was for procreation only and there are still Christian groups proclaiming this. However, this is not what the Bible teaches. Sex was created by God to populate (Genesis 1:28), to express unity (Genesis 2:24), to know your mate (Genesis 4:1), to express love (Genesis 24:67), to meet each other's needs (Genesis 24:67; Deuteronomy 24:5; 1 Peter 3:7), to play (Proverbs 5:19; Song of Solomon 2:8-17; 4:1-16; Ecclesiastes 9:9), and to prevent sin (1 Corinthians 7:2-5). Intimacy also includes our being available to our spouse (1 Corinthians 7:3-5), and showing him or her undivided interest as an expression of love (Song of Solomon 4:16; 5:2). Thus, cherish your spouse, romance them, and allure them.

The real authenticity of our Lord, will enable us to build a real authenticity of love and respect, that will in turn build a "Wondrous Marriage!"

Key marriage tip: When love prevails in the midst of marriage, especially in times of strife and disagreement, it presents to God and each other a willingness to heal.

Key marriage tip: Pursuing love in the midst of one's toil is the irrefutable mark of a true follower of Jesus Christ!

The following are questions to challenge, inspire and equip you to be better in your commitment, love and marriage:

Read John 13:34-35—chaps14-15; Colossians 3:12-14

1. What does it mean to you that Love confirms the authenticity of Jesus? How does love confirm your authenticity?
2. How can love and friendship prevail in the midst of your marriage, especially in times of strife and disagreement?
3. How can you demonstrate love, even when you are hurt, broken, and tired?
4. How can you present yourself to God and to each other a willingness to heal?

5. What would your marriage look like when you are pursuing love in the midst of your toil? How is this the irrefutable mark of a true follower of Jesus Christ?
6. What can you do to make love prevail more in your marriage?

Keep spending time in prayer and commit to pray for your spouse when you first wake up, when you go to bed, and throughout the day!

Love confirms the authenticity of Jesus' followers! Does it confirm the authenticity of your marriage?

CHAPTER 4

Why God Made Marriage

Husbands, love your wives, just as Christ loved the church and gave himself up for her to make her holy, cleansing her by the washing with water through the word, and to present her to himself as a radiant church, without stain or wrinkle or any other blemish, but holy and blameless. Ephesians 5:25-27

Marriage is good and was instituted by God even before the *Fall*.

It is how we are designed to be and live. God made marriage, according to Scripture and various theologians like Augustine (A.D. 354-430), for three basic reasons. And First, marriage was created for procreation, to have children in a safe nurturing environment. Second, marriage is the place to practice our faith. Third, marriage is a sacrament, and for us Reformed people, this is translated to how we glorify God (Genesis 1:18-24; 2 Corinthians 5:7-9; 5:14-20).

Key marriage tip: Yes, you can! We can apply the love and forgiveness Christ gave us. This will allow us to do more, each being a helpmate to the other while growing in maturity and raising good and healthy children who love God and life—all becoming a precious family that is the anchor of the community and civilization.

Marriage is also a gift, where we can, in a mutually loving relationship, share our precious life experiences. He created this institution for our enjoyment and benefit. Marriage is also the union of two flawed, imperfect people who have been hurt by the sins of this world that can prepare for the hope of the next world. We can exercise our relational aspect of needing to be with another, of being relational and not alone. It is where we can live effectually with hope and feel and know and practice real, effectual love.

The Heart of Marriage

God wants our marriages to be centers of His redemptive work, lived out in unity and security. You become His display to others, His beacon of light. A marriage is two people coming together in a sinful world to form an intimate community—a family.

The family, starting with two and may expand, can be a platform for character development where the issues of life and faith with a life partner who has our best interest in mind are wrest. It is an area where we help each other, work out faults and hurts, growing in trust and building upon our relationship with God and each other. Family is the safe harbor where we are honest and help each other grow, leaving behind our self-centered nature and embracing another person. It helps us teach one another, grow in love, overcome obstacles, and celebrate victories.

This, for all in the family, is how we learn to love, grow in love, even when we fail in that love, then pick it up—continuing to communicate and commune with one another and with our Lord and Savior together.

God knows this will be difficult, but He knows it is doable, achievable, and even pleasant. He knows that we each think differently and are wired differently; in fact, many times we are in opposition. We grow up in different places with different experiences, and we come together with our bags of desires, expectations, burdens, fears, faults, hurts, and expectation for joy. We soon collide into each other's faults and our expectations crash into our spouse's expectations where we are dented with our disappointments because we missed God's signposts of love and His precepts on how to make this work. Yet, He is there; Christ is saying and staying while He seeks to help us do it right.

Our pride and refusal to make it work are what stand in the way.

This is our "mark," the prime characteristic that makes us friendly and connectable to others, and how we are to be known—by what Christ does with us and calls us to. We are to love one another—period! No strings attached! This is the mold for the form that we use to display God's love to the world (John 13:34-35; 15:13-17; Galatians 5:22; 1 John 2:10; 3:14-16)!

When we *love one another*, we prove and exhibit Christ!

Jesus showed His love by taking our place for the wrath and punishment of our sins. He kindly took our interests over His and paid that price through His sinless life and His sacrifice on our behalf. Love takes the initiative, as Christ did with us, and fosters the Fruit of the Spirit and brotherly love that must empower the Christian life and be the beacon for the life of a church! If not, something is terribly off!

The love that Jesus has for us is a kind hand outstretched to us.

'Love the Lord your God with all your heart and with all your soul and with all your mind and with all your strength.' The second is this: 'Love your neighbor as yourself.' There is no commandment greater than these. **Mark 12:30-31**

This comes from a crescendo of applications Christ gave to us by His work and gives us the precepts to practice with running the home with love. Conversely, anger, pride, and malice that creates our arguments and builds upon our hurt, resides in our behaviors and becomes a tightly hinged spring waiting to pounce into an escalation of our arrogance, criticism, defensiveness, and withdrawing. These can only be put off when we put on Christ.

Key marriage tip: Love is a journey and a process. You learn each of the characteristics of love, as knowing them, eternalizing them, accepting them, to practice them and allow the time in others to the learning curve. And remember, it is a continual adventure, not a destination.

A Christian home is a practice in placing Christ first and above all, and allowing His work in you to come through you and in your family. A family is a microcosm of the Church all united in Christ, with gifts and responsibilities united not only in blood and bond, but in a greater connection of who we are in Christ! God gives us this picture in Ephesians 5. How we are in our relationships is the indicator of how we are in our relationship with Christ.

A happy, affectionate Christ-centered family is not about power and control or about fears and usurping authority or rebelling from it. It is about His love flowing into each of the members, all in unison. This does not mean we do not have our ups and downs and problems, but we can create an atmosphere of trust and love as well as encouragement and support (Ephesians 5:22-6:9)!

Key marriage tip: Marriage is not a 50-50 split; rather it is a call to go the extra mile. If you only count your cost, then you are not counting on the Lord!

A real, effective Christian family will have Love at its core. This fruit will promote our ability to relate to all and to grow in all of our relationships to better others as well as ourselves.

What if I did it all wrong?

Marriage is a wonderful and extraordinary relationship with that special person that God has foreordained. This is meant to be a good relationship that will bring glory to God by reflecting the relationship between Jesus and His bride, the church! If you are not married, do not be afraid to make the right decision, even if you have been in a relationship for years and are about to get married. If you know they are Mr. or Miss Wrong, get out; your time has not been wasted! Now is the time to move on! And, if you did get married to the wrong one, our call is simple: Be willing to work on it. After all, a spark was there that got you together in the first place.

In Christ, you will be able to turn your potential tragedy into a triumph. Even if you did not follow Biblical precepts and married Mr. or Mrs. Wrong, he or she is the right person now. We have to be willing to connect and make it work. If there is abuse or severe dysfunction, please get professional help immediately.

God calls us to work from your heart using the best of your abilities to bring out the best in others. That also means to bring out the best in your loved ones. In so doing, we glorify God when we endure with our faith and character—no matter what we might face or experience. The chief purpose for Christians, above all else, is to glorify God. Marriage is the best platform to make this happen (Luke 22:42; John 17:22; Ephesians 4:1-16; Colossians 3:18-4:1).

Christ is our great example of respect and endurance; He endured and suffered for you, He took your place in God's wrath, and as a sinless, innocent person, went to the cross for us all. We follow in His steps—not for our salvation, as it has already been given to the Christian—but to show another picture to those who are watching us. We exemplify Him by being a good example! Why? He has healed and saved us, so we need to trust Him out of our gratitude, and allow Him to be our Shepherd, Guardian, and Lord over all.

See your marriage as a platform to *reverence for the Lord.*

This passage in Ephesians states that Christ loved the church, not *because it was holy, but in order to make it holy*!

You and your spouse—as Christians—are the church. We are not only called to find the person who is best for us, but also to work at keeping that relationship within the parameters of love, submission, and commitment. Even if you made the wrong choice through impatience, wrong thinking, lust, and/or sin, you still have the call and opportunity to make it right and to make it work with the mate you have! Commit to memory that something special that got you together in the first place, and it can be rekindled into a roaring fire. This glorifies our Lord (Ephesians 5:22-6:9).

What God wants for our Marriage

Christ our Lord wants two people who do not always see everything the same and who are wired differently to come together to show each other the love that Christ displayed and taught us.

Marriage is the place for us to relinquish our pride and love, to forgive and to flourish. We will be hurt and disappointed, stepped on and humiliated, yet we must persevere in our love even when it does not make sense or if we feel that our spouse does not deserve our love or effort or does not appreciate or notice it.

To know and practice love! Love is not a mere feeling or a matter of the heart, although love is accompanied by feelings and heart. Love is the coal-tender (the train car that is behind the steam locomotive that carries the fuel) led by the will and mind; it must persevere and preserve. If we just let our hearts lead us, we will fail. It would just be a fuel car and a match with no engine to pull it in the right direction. Our marriage will blow up and fail because *the heart wants what the heart wants* and what it wants is just gas and a match, not always good or beneficial for us.

Key marriage tip: Yes, you can love and be loved, and we can make it work with the key of knowing Christ and applying His real, effectual love and grace.

Here are some questions to challenge, inspire and help equip you to be better in your commitment, love and marriage:

Read **Mark 12:30-31;** Ephesians 5:25-27; John chaps14-15

1. Do you see your marriage as a gift, where you can live in a mutually loving relationship, share your precious life experiences? How so? What needs to be worked on?
2. The warning signs of marriage is when one or both are feeling lonely, worried, hurt or troubled. How is yours? Be in prayer!
3. The anger signs of marriage that will cause dysfunction and divorce is pride, arrogance, condescension, and contempt, or withdraw! How is yours? What can you do to solve and prevent these diseases?
4. How can you make your marriage more intimate, communal community, a safe harbor? What can you do to not stay angry and bitter? Be in prayer!
5. What can you do to be centers of His redemptive work, lived and played out to bring unity and security? How would this improve your marriage?

Keep spending time in prayer and commit to pray for your spouse when you first wake up, when you go to bed and throughout the day!

CHAPTER 5

God's Model for Marriage

'Do not seek revenge or bear a grudge against one of your people, but love your neighbor as yourself. I am the LORD.' Leviticus 19:18

God has His best plan and model for us.

Why do we have such a "difficult" time applying this? Our basic problem is that we are flawed people who have been hurt and damaged by one another; sometimes, we can't see what we are to do with that hurt. We become hurting people who hurt those who are close to us and love us. We can hurt ourselves by overeating, we can drink alcohol, we can seek medication or some substance or person to soothe us; maybe we fight and return the hurt with more force than what we received.

Key marriage tip: Help each other realize they are irreplaceable. Encourage and inspire one another's hopes and dreams and to live the adventure of life well.

Maybe we leave behind what God has made and seek something different. Unfortunately, any of these solutions only makes the initial problem worse, bigger, more hurtful; no problem is solved and others are created. We need to see that our pride is in the way and our hearts are going in the wrong direction. This is evil, and we must let it go. We must recognize our need to be loved and make the allowance for this. We need to see that our spouses are not our enemies; he/she needs to be respected and loved—loved, no matter what. It is necessary for us to see beyond the hurt, to move beyond. No doubt, this takes effort and courage.

God's view of Marriage

My command is this: Love each other as I have loved you. Greater love has no one than this, that he lay down his life for his friends. You are my friends if you do what I command. I no longer call you servants, because a servant does not know his master's business. Instead, I have called you friends, for everything that I learned from my Father I have made known to you. You did not choose me, but I chose you and appointed you to go and bear fruit—fruit that will last. Then the Father will give you whatever you ask in my name. This is my command: Love each other. John 15:12-17

Our challenge is this. Christ's love was expressed not only in words, but also in His sacrificial death. We may not have to sacrifice ourselves literally for our spouses, but we have to see that real love *is* sacrificial. Simply and profoundly put, we are to love in this way, placing the other first!

We may see our marriages as dry, dysfunctional, or stuck—maybe they are. We tried to change our spouses and realized that would never work. They, in turn, tried to change us; it didn't work. We tried to manipulate, woo, and/or attack—all led to discontent. We wanted contentment. We are frustrated, confused, and disillusioned. The giddiness and excitement we had as an engaged or newly married couple has since dissipated; it seems that we might just be left with despair, divorce. Please do not despair. There is hope! You can have love if you are willing to love and be loved!

We face challenges and our inclination may be to give up, move on; unfortunately, what we give up is what God has made as His best for us.

We must have the desire to make marriage work regardless of how we feel or what we can see. We have to *want* to be in a good marriage to *have* a good marriage.

We can't allow our pettiness—even an accumulation of it—to overwhelm and consume us. It all comes down to what we learned earlier: We have to realize *we can have better!* *We have to lead our hearts and not be led by them!* Look up and see our Savior. Allow Him to lead your will and heart. This is the essential aspect to growth: to be willing to grow, to be willing to work it out, to seek forgiveness and reconciliation just as Christ did with your very soul. We must pursue our spouses with real love—not pettiness and retribution. Lay down your burdens (your baggage, if you will) at the feet of Jesus, and ask Him to lead you. No matter what we have been through, we can turn this around if we keep our focus on the Lord and let Him work in and through us.

The question: Do you love and value Christ as Lord? If so, you are on the right track and more than halfway there.

Now you need to take His love and let it infuse you so it can come out of you. You need to have a desire to grow in your faith and knowledge to lead your heart effectively. We have to take our nuptials seriously, be willing to work for it just as a soldier is willing to die for his or her country. Are you willing to live for your Lord and your spouse? We can be committed to solving our problems. If not, we will fail in our marriages and disappoint our Lord and Savior!

Key marriage tip: Show concern and care. Ask about their day. Who did they talk to, what did they learn? Speak without jealousy or condescending remarks or attitude. Listen! <u>Care enough to hear and uplift</u>. Listen first before offering any ideas or solutions. Put the care into your spouse as you would put into a nice car or a pair of shoes!

We, as Christians, are to set our sights and our focus upon Christ as Lord, who raised us to new life, for this is our authentic reality and Truth. As two children of God are placed together, this becomes paramount for an effectual marriage and a home filled with love and contentment. Yes, you will still have the ups and downs, mistakes will be made and hurts formed. However, you are on a journey together. You can weather these storms together, work together, and you can survive and even thrive.

Keep this in mind, a real effectual marriage is never just about you as husband or wife; it is all about us pointing to Christ—He is the pasture to whom we live and lead others, too. He is the Living Water we drink from and lead others to. We lead our family to point to Christ, this is especially paramount for the man, to take the lead. We are to fully, wholeheartedly trust in Christ, who sits at God's right hand in honor and power in the reality of Heaven. We need to demonstrate our trust, so we as Christians are the examples of a great marriage to the world. We are the product testers, and the forerunners. Why? We are heaven bound; we are to set our thoughts and hopes on Him so others can see where we lead (Colossians 3:15-17).

What does this all come down to? The key to being a good spouse, to being a great love is to get this one simple thing from 1 Peter 3,...*in your hearts set apart Christ as Lord.*

The call for marriage is to revere, to respect, to worship, to place first Christ because He is Lord. Only then can we relate to and edify one another properly. If we can do this, we can serve and glorify our Lord and build our families and in turn build His Kingdom well. If we do not, we build dysfunction from our pride, torture our children, and thus disrespect our Lord. Sounds harsh, but this is true. I have seen this not only in myself when I lose focus, but I have seen it countless times by failing families and marital disputes who just do not get it and ruin their family and legacy (1 Peter 3:13-15).

How do we do maintain the focus?

Let Christ fill our thoughts and take hold of our will so we need not give a thought to earthly troubles and fears. We need to not buy into our own discontent or fears, when we should be demonstrating Christ, so our family members are looking to Him. We are in Christ; we died to Him, and He is our genuine world and life; we share in His glory. We can put sin and our sinful ways of pride and condescension to death, those earthy wants and needs that are bad and cause harm to others and us.

A profile of a Christian home. We are called to live higher, not in money or power, rather to have nothing to do with evil or sin or any kind of anger, greed, bad language, lying, or any thoughts of impurity or idolatry. People look to the Christian home to set a tone, to be examples as shepherds to lead and care for them, not as examples on how to fight and fall. These things hurt God's heart and cause misery for many generations; we do not want that. When we have received His grace and forgiveness, why would we go back to what hurts others and us? Strip off this old nature of sin, set aside your pride and hurts so you can put on His nature of fruitfulness and renewal by clothing yourselves in His goodness with your new nature within you that He created. Only then do we lead our families and build our homes with authenticity and gratefulness, always pointing to Christ as He is real and true and lives in us all.

Key marriage tip: Marriages break up when you stop sharing, stop communicating, stop listening, and start assuming. Remember, communication is a 'requirement,' an 'always' and 'have to'. It is not an elective aspect, and you have to work on it.

This is all about living the Christian life out as best as we can with His empowerment and grace. We are to make Christ primary in in our lives in order to receive His blessings and empowerment in the home and in the Church; only when we do this, can pass it on to others! Jesus is our focus and attention rather than our own agendas. In keeping Christ as our Focus, we will have a wondrous marriage and lead lives of distinction, maturity, and character (Matthew 6:33; Romans 6:1-14; Ephesians 2:1-10).

Key marriage tip: You must get a grasp on grace and how Christ loves us; if you do not, you will only live with problems, and you will regress in distress.

Make a covenant to choose to walk with surrendered, Lordship faith in Jesus Christ: "I choose to be filled with His Spirit. Since I choose to be filled with His Spirit, **I choose to love and honor my spouse!**

Questions to challenge, inspire and help equip you to be better in your commitment, love and marriage:

Read Leviticus 19:18; John chaps14-15

1. Have you tried to change or manipulate your spouse? When did you realize that it would never work? If not, what can you do to stop?
2. What can you do to prevent the instinct or inclination to give up and move on?
3. Do you love and value Christ as Lord? How can you take His love and let it infuse you so that you are living Christ's love and sharing it?
4. Christ's love was expressed not only in words, but in His ultimate deed. How can His love for you, motivate you to be a better 'lover' to your spouse?
5. You can have love if you are willing to love and be loved! How can you be more loving and living in your marriage?

I encourage you to keep spending time in prayer and commit to praying for your spouses when you wake up, when you go to bed, and throughout the day! Approach your spouses about praying together—just 5 minutes a day for starters. If your spouses aren't open to this, please do not push or feel alone— take it to Our Lord in prayer.

CHAPTER 6

Marriage where Real Love is Practiced

Be very careful, then, how you live—not as unwise but as wise, making the most of every opportunity, because the days are evil. Therefore do not be foolish, but understand what the Lord's will is. Do not get drunk on wine, which leads to debauchery. Instead, be filled with the Spirit, speaking to one another with psalms, hymns, and songs from the Spirit. Sing and make music from your heart to the Lord, always giving thanks to God the Father for everything, in the name of our Lord Jesus Christ. Ephesians 5:15-20

Marriage must be the place where real love is practiced.

As I stated earlier, most people do not know what *love* or *the heart* are all about. *Heart,* in biblical language, means our 'inner will' where one's desires and conflicts reside. It is also associated with the peace in our hearts that makes peace with others and peace in the family and church that influences the world. Our heart is what controls and rules us most of the time.

Yet, as Christians, we are to be directed by God's principles, His character, and the Holy Spirit's leading, applying these to ourselves and relationships—especially with our spouses. Being led by the Word of God will enable us to be filled with the Spirit of God; they go together—inseparable. One cannot be effective in life, ministry, or marriage without both. You cannot say the Holy Spirit fills you by being emotionally ecstatic or erratic while you ignore God's Word and hurt your spouse.

Key marriage tip: Real love is cherished. This makes the marriage work, and you have to choose to do it and play it forward. This love in action must take us beyond ourselves and into the other person. When we fully understand what love is and dedicate ourselves to practice it, then we will have a thriving and content marriage!

It is not the heart that gives us hope, reason, purpose, meaning, and motivation; our Lord does that through His Word that we receive. The growth from this gift influences our mindsets and is evident in our attitudes, outlooks, and actions in all facets of life. Our choices dictate the consequences, and we will either fill our lives with hope or despair, joy or discontent, gratitude or ingratitude, contentment or dissatisfaction—all dependent upon our willingness to lead our hearts right.

A real mature Christian is willing to be controlled and filled by Christ and not by apprehension, selfishness, turmoil, damaged past, or uncertainty.

(Acts 2:4; 4:8, 31; 6:3; Romans 8:9; 1 Corinthians 7:32-35; 12:13; Ephesians 5:8-6:9, Colossians 3:19-4:1)

Love Confirms the Authenticity of Marriage!

Cherish! The type of love that is to be practiced is the kind the Bible speaks of. This love becomes 'our treasure,' an unconditional love that helps fuel one another's desire to return that love. To give a picture of what 'cherished' means, I need to bombard you with more adjectives, and while that still will not fully color in the picture, it is that deep. It means to hold our love dear, so we don't just feel, but honor and show and our affection. In so doing, we will be able to cultivate care and affection with tenderness. This is like the cup to First Corinthians Thirteen.

Respect! This is the other essential aspect of love is respect. A wife respects her husband and can show him value because she feels protected and cherished. This is like the saucer for the cup to First Corinthians Thirteen.

To cherish our wife is the most important call for the husband and the most important need for the wife. To respect is the most important call for the wife and the most important need for the husband. When these are in synergy, the magic of marriage happens.

In practice, the husband receives his value and honor by the respect and feels enabled to love. The wife responds to the love because she knows she is cared for and cherished. This kind of real effectual Love is often, the husband loves and the wife responds with respect and honor and so conversely. When we do this, then your relationship will vastly improve! This happens when we are being *imitators of God* (Ephesians 5:1-2; John 14:15).

Most people look for a mate to complete them—yes, even Christians. The problem with that is, no human can fulfill this role that only Christ can. Jesus completes us. Can any human touch the completeness of Christ Jesus? No. Thus, we can't expect someone or something else to do that. We will only be disappointed and discouraged. What we do is become complete in Christ and point others to His completion. In so doing, we complement and inspire and extol our spouse, as we are both 'complete' in Him. How do we do this? Gratitude promotes peace and secures a content heart, whereas sin and turmoil become cancerous and adversely affect others around us (Psalm 32; 51; Colossians 2:2, 3:15-17).

By the same token, most people (even most Christians) do not know what real love really is. Or what it means to be complete, as His love does this. We may know 1 Corinthians 13 and may even have memorized it, but may I dare you to ask yourself,

Do you practice it?

Do you know what those words mean?

Do you know what love really is?

Do you know what love is <u>not</u> is as important as what love is?

Most of us have this backwards. We think we know the answers; in fact, we do not. We may not know that Love is more of an act of our will than it is a feeling. Love is a choice. Yes, it comes as a feeling, but feelings are fleeting.

Do you know that love is not about what you want or desire? Rather, it seeks what the other person needs.

Did you know that real love takes us beyond ourselves and into the other person?

When you fully understand what love is and dedicate yourselves to practicing real Biblical love, you will have a thriving and content marriage. It may take time, but it will unfold because you are unfolding what God has for you and placing His principles in play. You have to be willing to not just guard your heart to listen to it; you must lead it to the right wellbeing and prosperity, and that is with the one God has brought you.

Following God's plan is not easy. The world's way is!

However, when we indulge in the world's way, the *easy* will quickly turn into *hurt* and *chaos*! So, the *easy* ends up being very difficult indeed!

God, without a doubt, has a wonderful plan for you, but that plan will take effort, time, commitment, risk, and self surrender. It goes from what you may think is good and right to what really is good and right. Take to heart that these principles of real love will work and will enable you to find the heart of your marriage and make it wondrous. It may happen quickly, or it may take years to get it going. Remember, God is patient in His love for you! Are you patient in your love for your spouse?

Key marriage tip: You must have respect for your spouse, even when they do not deserve it! The most important things: a man needs is respect and a woman needs to be cherished. If you can't respect, you can't have a healthy loving marriage. Get help and work on developing respect, but know how much God loves and cares for you both.

Remember the characteristics of love from 1 Corinthians 13 and apply them to your marriage. Focus on the patience. At the same time, do not sit on the couch and wait. You have to step up and take risks and endure hostility and rejection. You have to go where he or she is. We need to be working on ourselves; we must be open and vulnerable. If you are not willing to take a risk or work on yourself, you will be trading a little hurt from the rejection and pride for the unwillingness to build your character, and that will result in broken relationships and/or a lifetime of hurt and loneliness. You will miss out on what God has for you and your marriage.

Recovering from Hurt

Sometimes we do all we can and our marriages still do not improve. To be honest, after over 30 years of doing counseling and decades of research, this is rare. Yet, it happens. Sometimes, there are chemical imbalances in the brain and one can't control their thoughts and actions well and refuse medical help. Sometimes, people are so damaged they can't get beyond their hurts. And, in most of these cases, they also refuse to get help and choose to stay in their dysfunction. If they will not get help, and you can't force them, then you get it for yourself.

Key marriage tip: Recognize each other's boundaries! You know the buttons; do not push them! Instead, honor and value them as God's child to respect them enough to love them enough.

Allow me to speak to you as a pastor. I am so sorry you have been hurt. I know how you feel as I have experienced hurt too many times. In this, sometimes it is very difficult to fathom a love and trust that is pure.

No, we are not to allow others to hurt us, regardless of what may be deemed 'culturally' or trying to be the good Christian! This does not mean we are to be gullible or foolhardy or take mistreatment or exploitation because this is not detached from God's other precepts of wisdom and discernment. It does not say we are to remain in an abusive situation; rather, believe the best in others until proven otherwise (Proverbs 14:15; Romans 5:5; 1 Peter 4:8).

Basically, Christ is the One we trust and then He enables us to receive His love and resend it or replicate it onto others. However, you are God's special and precious child. You are not to repay evil with evil. You are to love as Christ loves us. And, you are most assuredly not to be used or abused. There is no excuse for maltreatment. If you are in danger, get out. If you are being abused, get out. Please, get out. Get help from friends, neighbors, your church, legal authorities, and/or organizations who provide help.

God also tells us to have boundaries and stay away from someone who hurt you, even a family member. So exercise discernment and be cautious; if the person does not give back trust or hurts, follow Matthew 18 and get help from a trusted pastor or church elder. The takeaway of a love that trusts is this: What we need to learn as Christians is that real love is not meant to fulfill our own needs; rather, it is a gift of grace by faith. It allows us not to be tied to what others do for or have done for us!

If you are not being hurt, then stick with it and focus on God's timing.

We can be supportive, loyal, hopeful, and trusting—this is our example to others in a hurting world that need to see it. We trust in Christ and have the faith and confidence to let His love flow in and through us to others so we can trust them without expecting anything back.

What will this do in our relationships?

We will not jump to conclusions, be cynical, or be suspicious, on the ready to denounce or domineer. Faith that is not powered by Christ, but practiced by our worldly "trust" or by our damage is useless, false, dead, and can even be demonic.

(Psalm 37:23; John 13:1; 15: 3,13; Romans 3:24; 5:1-5;9:3; 14:23; 1 Corinthians 9:22; 16:14; Galatians 2:20; Colossians 3:12-17; 1 Thessalonians 4:9-10;5:8-18; 1 Timothy 1:5; Hebrews 11:6; 1 John 5:12)

God does not want us to be controlled by the past or to be fearful or cowardly.

We are to learn from our experiences and grow from them, but not be tied to them so they become our identity. We have been born again in Christ; our old life is old, and it is no longer who we are. Thus, we are to grow closer to Him and be an example to others who are still in the old life without allowing them to influence and entice us. Keep in mind that our hopes are not hinged on what others have done or can do; our hope is in Christ alone.

Key marriage tip: Be grateful to the Lord, be patient, and remember real love is a choice—you have to work at it. Our maturity and growth in Christ will facilitate this, then you can be better committed to making it work, no matter what.

Questions to challenge, inspire, and equip you to be better in your commitment, love and marriage:

Read Psalm 32; 51; 1 Corinthians 7:32-35; 13; Colossians 2:2, 3:15-17

1. Love Confirms the Authenticity of Marriage! How does this look in yours? What do you need to do?
2. What cultivates your mindset that influences your attitudes, outlooks, and actions in life and in the family?
3. As Christ demonstrated, real love is sacrificial. So what can you do to be better are showing love to your spouse, even when they do not deserve it?
4. What do you need to do to be led by the Word of God? How will this enable your marriage to be filled with the Spirit of God?
5. How does your spiritual growth help you with real hope, reason, purpose, meaning, and motivation? How will this affect your marriage?

Keep spending time in prayer and commit to pray for your spouse when you first wake up, when you go to bed and throughout the day! Now, also see if you can pray with your spouse, too—at least 5 minutes a day to start. If they are not open to it, do not push it; just pray for it.

CHAPTER 7

Cherish and Respect

Jesus replied: "'Love the Lord your God with all your heart and with all your soul and with all your mind.' This is the first and greatest commandment. And the second is like it: 'Love your neighbor as yourself.' All the Law and the Prophets hang on these two commandments." Matthew 22:37-40

Love and respect are the two essential components of a healthy marriage—you can't have one without the other.

A love that cherishes and a respect that values are the key essential precepts for building vibrant, healthy and affectionate marriages. We get this from God's Word from the passages on love. This is a prime example of 'agape' love and how to live it—sacrificial and effectual. The original word in Hebrew and Latin for *cherish* meant to heat up something so that it is softened to be workable, like smelting a metal, so it is workable for the blacksmith. It is also used as a word to keep warm like a bird covering its young under its wings in protection and embracing warmth. Each of these example is something of value to be tended to and protected. The message of *cherish* is that God works in us because He values us and cares for us, loves us, so He works us so we are bendable and flexible to one another. It is a call to be as He is with us.

As Christians, and even more so in marriage, we are called to protect and be affectionate, being kind and nurturing to our spouse.

(Deuteronomy 22:6; Proverbs 4:2-9; 19:8; Ephesians 5:28-30; 1 Thessalonians 2:6-8)

We are to revere God because He cherishes us by His grace and care. Then, He tells us to play it forward.

Key marriage tip: Families that pray together, stay together and are tighter.

Being respectful of and cherishing someone are both responses from God's love to us and how we react in that love to one another. These are the key cultivation tools for nurturing and caring that God gives us to form us in Him. This nurturing compounds and builds with time and kindheartedness to build up our vital relationships. Imagine what this means for your family!

Our love to our spouse is predicted by God's love to us.

This means we respond to others by how God has interacted in us. Jesus loves you and your spouse, therefore you can take that same love because they are worthy in God's sight to receive your love and respect; we are to deeply love and passionately care for our spouses as Jesus does for us. We are to keep it up for a lifetime even, joy and purpose in it—finding happiness and contentment, too.

Key marriage tip: Yes, we need to detox from our day, but, do not come home just tired and plop in front of the TV, rather greet your family and spend time with them first. Need to wind down? Then, spend 10 minutes in your car or place of work or school and pray before entering your home.

Cherish means a more direct effectual cultivation and application of love.

This is why the King James translators chose "charity" in First Corinthians thirteen for love, as it refers to *cherish* over just saying love. Charity now means the act of giving to a foundation or cause. But then, charity came from 'Middle English,' with roots in French and Latin meaning *dearness* as used for "Christian love." They didn't choose "charity" because it was a cheaper word or a less passionate word for the emerging Victorian age; rather, it was more dear, a more powerful application for a word that demonstrates how we are to love one another from the root word of love of being sacrificial, so it takes us to our loved ones beyond measure.

Saying "love" is just as confusing then as it is today. Something more was needed—a word of action, denoting a deeper, more treasured protection, and true application that takes us to a deeper level of the relationship. This is also why John Wycliffe used and promoted "charity" in one of the first Translations other that Latin, in his early English Bible in 1382. For Wycliffe and for us, "charity" which now comes to mean "cherish," is not a mere word; it is a call of our Lord to love as He loved us.

(Deuteronomy 6:5; Matthew 22:37-40; 1 Corinthians13; Ephesians 5:29; 1 Thessalonians 2:7)

Key marriage tip: Before you give up on your spouse, try harder, pray, and think it through.

Look at it this way, when you apply the word "cherish", you are applying God's model for love as depicted in 1 Corinthians 13. This is a love that builds up and takes our hearts and attitude beyond the confines of our pride or hurt or will or plans. This is so we can hold dear our loves ones, even when they hurt us. We can nurture them and be tender. We can be devoted to their time and needs even though they may disappoint us. We can have a deeper care and adoration, even when times get tough (1 John 4:8).

...To have and to hold from this day forward, for better, for worse, for richer for poorer, in sickness and in health, to love and to cherish...

The reason why cherish is in the classic marriage vows is because of the previously said reasons. It calls us to be kinder and deeper than the word of 'love'. *"To have and to hold..., to love and to cherish, till death us do part,..."* This way, in public, we have the call and accountability to hold dear our spouse, and this is a reminder for others to do the same.

Key marriage tip: Before you criticize or blame, take some time out to pray and think it through first.

To cherish our wife is the most important call for the husband and the most important need for the wife.

Cherishing for the man is a little different. Men like, perhaps even need the admiration, aspect of love. For men, they are held dear, when they are respected and listened to. Thus, kindness is demonstrating admiration by showing they are of value for being in your life. Men see love from the appreciation angle for the things they do. Women feel loved and cherished for how they are treated. For men and women, love is thoughtful and kind and says "Thank you" and means it.

To respect is the most important call for the wife and the most important need for the husband. When these are in synergy, the magic of marriage happens, contentment is in the house.

R.E.S.P.E.C.T.

Respect is the essential relationship-building tool to hone a man up in the Lord. Why? Respect means approval. For men, this means they have been accepted, they have a purpose because the wife has shown them favor. In the Hebrew it means to lift up a person's face, meaning give favorably. That is why the Hebrew implication is that the women moves the neck, meaning they guide his head in the direction the family need and goes. It is like a helpmate that sets a tone for a person to see where they can go and how they can be, because you are pointing them there (Romans 2:11; Galatians 2:6; 1 Thess 4:9-12; James 2:1,9; 1 Peter 2: 17).

Key marriage tip: Have something to say? Before you talk, make sure you are listening. No one, even your spouse, cares what you have to say if they are not cared for and heard first.

Why should we respect our spouse who has proven to not be worthy, is an idiot, makes me mad? Because God tells us they are worth it just as you are to Him.

As we revere God, we can accept and honor His children that He declares us worthy. That means your spouse, too. God wants us to treat our spouse in a worthy manner because He says they are worthy—even when they are not. By treating them as God treats us, our spouses, and we, might just step up.

(Psalm 139:13-16; Jeremiah 29:11; Matthew 6:25-34; 10:31; Romans 5:8; Ephesians 1:3-4; 2:4-9)

What this does is amazing. It builds trust, contentment, and mutual cooperation by real loving and kindness. The wife motivates her spouse to step up.

Sometimes, this is a long process. When we are respected, we feel accomplished, good, and purposeful. This creates a representation of God at work, a 'living picture' of a Christian family saved by grace and then modeling God's work to one another. It is our secret weapon that should never be secret as it moves people forward to deeper maturity and fruitfulness.

Key marriage tip: Do not always be blaming, criticizing, complaining and nagging, as these rotten fruits will never work. Show love by being kind and being an example with encouragement.

When the husband feels worthy, they pass on worthy to their spouse. Because we are cherished, we can respect. Because we are respected, we can cherish. This is reciprocal and effectual.

Respect in application means to be considerate by treating the husband with the greatest of care and love, because God gave them to you and they are worthy of that mandate. The wife's respect is a response to the husband's cherishing! Because the husband loves, cares, and puts his wife's best interests first, the wife submits, and he earns her devotion. Thus, cherishing and respecting are mutual and communal and exhibit all of the qualities of biblical character in the Christian home.

This motivates us to be good, do good, have morality, and consistency. Respect for the male is the hallmark of encouragement and approval, so we do the right thing. This impacts our connection to one another and our care for one another.

God does not want us stuck in our hurts so we build resentment.

We have to let go and honor one another, in the home and in public. Men and women need to feel safe and secure. Being respectful creates a shield of protection so one will not hurt the other or throw one under the proverbial bus (Job. 36:13; James 3:8-10; 1 Peter 2:17).

Key marriage tip: You do not have to be in control, only The Sovereign Lord is in control…Unless you created the universe, let it go and allow your control to be yielded over to the Lordship of Christ. Your life and marriage will vastly improve.

Allow me to say this a different way. As the husband cherishes the wife, she sets a tone from feeling cared for, so she will respect him. Because the husband is being respected, he feels accepted, important, and desires to evermore love her. Thus, for the husband to cherish his wife is to be our utmost responsibility, and done with care. And the wife is to respect and be a showcase of contentment. Both are forms of love, a call to careful, steadfast affection for like caring for a precious, priceless object (1 Timothy 1:15; 2:2; 4:9-10).

If you want your home content, then cultivate affection for one another and we do this by:

1. **Practicing real love means we will cherish our spouse!**
2. **Practicing real respect means we will value our spouse!**

Two more things we will discuss so that you can seal the deal:

3. **Guard against lust; focus on your spouse, not others!**
4. **Control your pride or it will control your home for sin!**

Practice these and you will be on the winning side of faith, family life, and harmony!

We cannot have the approval of God in our marriages when we are not reverencing Him and following through by treating one another with love and respect that He gives us and calls us to (Psalm 8:4-5; 66:18; Hebrews 12:9).

Key marriage tip: You do not have a legitimate need to impress others. A real impression is not what you have; rather how you are—Fruit of the Spirit.

The distinction of a the Christian home must be how we love, care for, and value one another. These principles are also the essential keys that build a great church.

Key marriage tip: You do not have to be always right. Let it go, and focus on being right in Christ!

A true marriage is a 'covenant marriage.' This means we go beyond the civil contract from the State, and we see our marriage as instituted from God, by God, because He reconciled us to Himself and call us to be reconcilers to one another as man and wife, a family under and for God's glory. This will create the synergy for the foundation of family and a lifelong fruitful relationship.

Consider this: Without the right attitude and perspective on life, without glorifying God and following His Will, you will not find the real, quality love relationship in your life! You will be taking a big gamble on losing out on what is priceless and precious.

Questions to challenge, inspire, and equip you to be better in your commitment, love, and marriage:

Read Deuteronomy 6:5; Matthew 22:37-40; Ephesians 5:15-18; 1 Thessalonians 4:9-12; 1 Timothy 1:15; James 3:8-10; 1 Peter 2:17; 1 John 4:8

1. What are the keys to a successful marriage? What have been your observations about real love and being respectful?
2. How do you feel when you are cherished? How do you think your spouse will feel?
3. How is real love about cherishing your spouse? How have you succeeded in this? How have you failed? What will you commit to do now?
4. How is real respect about valuing your spouse? How have you succeeded in this? How have you failed? What will you commit to do now?
5. What gets in the way of love and valuing being practiced in your home? What can you do to refocus on God's covenant and care over your feelings, failures or hurts?
6. How does pride become such a destroyer of families? Have you seen this happen? What can you do about it?
7. What will you do to value your spouse more?

CHAPTER 8

God's Way of Building a Great Marriage

And do this, understanding the present time. The hour has come for you to wake up from your slumber, because our salvation is nearer now than when we first believed. The night is nearly over; the day is almost here. So let us put aside the deeds of darkness and put on the armor of light. Let us behave decently, as in the daytime, not in orgies and drunkenness, not in sexual immorality and debauchery, not in dissension and jealousy. Rather, clothe yourselves with the Lord Jesus Christ, and do not think about how to gratify the desires of the sinful nature. Romans 13:11-14

To grow a wondrous marriage, we have to be willing to learn about real love, and we must understand that Christianity is about growth.

It starts with the profession of faith and conversion from our old selves into the new with Christ; this faith keeps building into maturity. The process of Sanctification comes into play here, especially in the midst of our relationships. At the same time, we have to be on guard against any sin, especially *dissension and jealousy* as these are marriage killers.

Key marriage tip: Laugh! Do not be afraid to laugh. In the best, happiest and long-lasting marriages, the couples laughed a lot. So, do not take yourself too seriously; be able to laugh!

There are times where you cannot meet all of the needs of your marriage partner, nor should you. Let your needs be determined by Biblical values and precepts. That other person you love needs to be discipled and growing in the right direction, as do you. They may need correction, you may need correction. They may need to change, and you may need to change. In most situations, it is both! Therefore, a balance has to occur between fulfilling their needs and fulfilling the right needs. Nevertheless, the bottom line, the call of God in love is to put them before yourself. You are not to be selfish or manipulative or have hidden agendas, and neither should they. And, of course, this takes a lifetime to work on.

Of course, there will be times we want to control or change them, but we have to be willing to repeal those selfish desires of our hearts in favor of their desires.

A Biblical relationship, one between God and us and with each other, will take the focus off you and put it on what can be empowered and/or invested in the other person. With God, the surrender of our will goes along to build our spiritual and our relational lives. Therefore, you have to discern through God's Word and prayer, *Where is my error between what I want, what I am called to* and that of a real friendship marriage with love. It can be different for each person (John 14-15; Galatians 2:20-21; Philippians 3:10).

Scripture tells us to *put off*, to *rid yourselves* of what will hurt us and others.

To 'put off' means to take the focus off ourselves and point to Christ. It is easy in concept, but takes a lifetime to do. This, in the Greek language, is an illustration of putting on armor for battle and then taking it off when the battle is over. As Christians, our battles are not to be with one another, especially a loved one. Rather, the battles are to be with what hurts us; the battle is finished when we are called to our eternal home.

Key marriage tip: You need to know the difference between saying you are a friend and being a friend. People with friends are also persons who are friend-makers because they listen. Your spouse has a deep need to be listened to. And, you need to be their best friend!

The image is to put off sin and embrace righteousness, as we are to be clothed in the Spirit, not in the world or in our desires. Also, this is a baptismal image as it was common practice to disrobe for the baptism and then put on new garments afterward if available for the point to be identified in Christ. This is accomplished by focusing on Christ, right thinking, and faith.

(Mark 1:5; Acts 7:58; Romans 13:12-14; Ephesians 4:24-25; 1 Peter 2:1)

We are to *put on love.* The verb for love (Greek: *agapete*) designates a continuous routine of action all of the time, not just when we feel like it. This it is to be continual. Real love is "symbiotic"—mutually loving toward each other to build and improve each one's relationship. In the context of a Christian marriage, a man loves a woman; she then submits because of his love. This submission is a love in itself that becomes as *"one flesh."* Literally, it means our souls are tied together. We will discuss and clarify more on this later. When this is actionable, our marriage becomes a real union. This from the Greek syntax—a union that should not be broken. Thus, our union with our spouse is meant to be a permanent as well as an intimate bond. How?! Let's look on some ideas from Scripture (Ephesians 2:4-7; 5:21-32).

Key ideas on what God has for us:

- We need to ask ourselves, *Am I willing to reduce myself down to merely "ME," as, who I am in Christ?* Are we willing to throw off our selfish desires, past hurts and pride? If so, we state and strive to be mature in Christ. Our relationships vastly improve!
- Are you determined enough to strip yourself of all that you are in the world, in your career, ministry, and your church, including what your friends and spouse think of you and what you think of yourself?
- Are you willing and determined to hand over your true self, your simple, naked self to God?

Once you are, then He can begin to do a greater work in you, and in others through you. Christ will immediately sanctify you completely, and your life will be free of what distracts you from His character and precepts. You can be determined and persistent toward glorifying God, and Christ as your Lord (1 Thessalonians 5:23-24)!

You can start by surrendering to Him in prayer (Galatians 2:20-21; Philippians 1:6; 3:10), *Lord, show me what sanctification means; help me live, as my life is yours.* He will show you!

Sanctification means being made one with Jesus. Sanctification is not something Jesus puts in you; it is He, Himself, in us (2 Corinthians 1:39). The understanding of Sanctification will allow you to lead your heart, to be discerning of yourself, and realize that no mere person can fulfill you! No ideal guy or gal will make you complete or fill a hole that only Christ can fill! No friend can take the place of God.

To completely change the black, dirty oil of our minds with the new, golden anointing oil of His love, we have to surrender ourselves to Christ.

When we become a Christian, the Spirit transforms us completely, all that we are, all that we do, our will, our plans, and our opportunities (2 Corinthians 3:18). However, this cannot happen unless we give our selfish heart and will over to His (Galatians 2:20-21)! The incentive for us to surrender to Christ is that His way is better than ours! This will directly translate into who we are, and how we are in all of our relationships. This means you can seek what is best for your spouse and marriage and be willing to work on both that relationship and on yourself.

Remember, most of the ideas people have about the heart, marriage, and love are artificial and insincere. The world's ways do not work and serve only to create strife and chaos.

We must be prepared to recognize the real fruits over the artificial ones. If not, when we think we have found love, we will only have lust and insincerity. These artificial fruits will turn into hate and indifference. When this happens, we will not be even close to expressing any kind of love, in any form. Do not let this happen to you and your marriage. Do not let yourself, or the ones you love, succumb to the myths of love and the leading of the heart that only produces false expectations, and leads into the dark, forbearing path of despair!

Key marriage tip: Be a person who extols—that is to affirm and encourage others—especially your family member. Be a person who takes the cue to be unto Christ and follow His example—to love and care with excellence and fortitude.

Songs and movies are nice entertainment; but, they are not the reality of life. The scripts and lyrics are often wrong; they do not work and often be harmful. Remember, love is a verb and choice to follow through. It is your choice to succeed or fail. Are you willing to succeed, knowing that so many countless millions of friendships end and marriages fail?

Being willing and able to work to understand yourself, love, and God's precepts will motivate you, and provide commitment to build your house of love. Being willing to make your spouse feel he or she is the priority and is special will make that home content, too.

What do I do?

I am saying this for your own good, not to restrict you, but that you may live in a right way in undivided devotion to the Lord. 1 Corinthians 7:35

We need to see life as an adventure with no time to waste. 1 Corinthians 7:32-35, gives us a picture of the magnitude and value of relationships with love in action, both in preparing for marriage and within marriage. The central focus, paying close attention to verse 35, is not being distracted by things that are false and misleading to us; rather, we are to focus on Christ and allow Him to provide us the motivation for leading our hearts to what brings godly living. His precepts must reign in us, so our attention is on the right track. If not, those myths and *cares* of the world—including the myths of love—will overtake us and bring us down into the world of bad decisions, leading to bad relationships and producing bad living.

What do I Not Do?

Try not to be irritated and irritating in return. This is usually done to manipulate and scheme to get our way over His Way. A husband is not to lead by being harsh, like a shepherd who is harsh. The sheep will refuse to go with him, and perhaps will even die. Rather, he leads and guides them in the right direction with gentleness; then the sheep (and wife) will follow him. The sheep do this out of a need to be protected, to be led to food and water that they cannot find on their own. Women also have the need to feel protected and cherished. Humans are to lead other humans to the precepts of His Word and character (James 3:11-14).

Remember, real Christian love is the turning of our backs to self-concerns, and facing forward to our relationships with family, friends, and neighbors. It is the surrender of our will to His. If love does not take us beyond our self-interests, what we have is lust and not authentic love!

Key marriage tip: If you are willing to live out the art of loving, then, you will keep your marriage alive and even thrive!

Questions to challenge, inspire, and equip you to be better in your commitment, love and marriage:

Read 1 Corinthians 13; 2 Corinthians 1:39; Galatians 2:20-21; Philippians 1:6; 3:10; 1 Thessalonians 5:23-24;

1. Why do you suppose that most of the ideas people have, Christians included, about the heart and love are artificial and insincere?
2. Are you willing to live out the art of loving, even when you do not feel like it or are hurt? How will this keep your marriage alive and even thrive?
3. What will it take or what will you do to get a grasp on God's amazing fullness of grace and how Christ loves us?
4. How will a biblical understanding of sanctification will help you to lead your heart?
5. What can you do to commit to love, commit to your spouse and keep working on your marriage?

If you do not have a mentor, now is the time to find one—preferably an older couple who have walked in faith for a significant period of time.

Be a builder, not a taker. Keep spending time in prayer and commit to pray for your spouse when you first wake up, when you go to bed and throughout the day! Now also see if you can pray with your spouse, too—at least 5 minutes a day to start. If they are not open to it, do not push it, just pray for it.

CHAPTER 9

Love in Marriage is Reciprocal and Continual

Follow God's example, therefore, as dearly loved children and walk in the way of love, just as Christ loved us and gave himself up for us as a fragrant offering and sacrifice to God. Ephesians 5:1-2

Building a Successful Marriage with Love and Respect

Remember this is not a book of my ideas; this is a book directing you to and reflecting for you God's precepts on building a great marriage. What I am doing is reading the Bible, doing some real research and extracting the precepts, practicing them and laying them out to you. I know the concepts are easy, the practice is tough and yet, it is doable even in harsh circumstances.

In contrast, the world considers marriage to be an avenue of satisfaction for the self. This view seems to be from the standpoint of seeking fulfillment in pleasure, companionship, what "I" can get out of it, and how "I" can benefit from it. These are, of course, parts of a relationship, but not the main parts. People get confused, disillusioned, and eventually give up on marriage because the above aspects are not being fulfilled to their satisfaction and expectations. They are negating what is really important and meaningful in building a marriage!

Key marriage tip: To create the best Christian marriage, this is essential: Men are to set a tone of love and be the head servant of the family; women are to respond to that love with respect and set the tone for a vibrant home.

If you want to be successful in life and marriage, you need to get this point: The primary purpose of marriage is not to please ourselves, but to glorify and serve God. Our desires and pleasures are not God's number one priority! Yes, God wants us to be joyful, happy, and content, but being happy means being focused on Him and not on our circumstances. To have a successful marriage, you must be aware of what you are getting into and prepare for it. The most important guarantee for marriage to work is to follow His principles from His Word, not what you think, want, or have experienced. Remember, God designed marriage and us. He knows best!

Marriage from the Perspective of Christ and the Church

In Ephesians 5:21-27, the theme is submission—a far cry from the American ideals of personal freedom and choice. However, consider this: Submission is not the tyrannical concept most of us harbor in our mind. Submission to the Lord is the truest form of freedom! It is a form of mutual respect. It allows us to be free, and to have the best flowing in and out of us. It is a safe harbor of smooth waters keeping us protected from the storms of wrong actions. It frees us from bad thinking that leads to bad choices which, in turn, leads to a life of misery and trouble! For a wife to respect her husband shows him unconditional love that helps fuel his desire to return the love. He receives his value and honor that is so important to a man. The wife responds because she knows she is cared for and cherished.

There is nothing more important to a man than to feel respected. There is nothing more important to a woman than to feel cherished!

Submission is not because of weakness or inferiority, or, that one is better than the other, but because God has placed, in the order of creation, the husband as head of the home, just as Christ is the head of the Church. They have different roles, yet each one is equal in the sight of God! The husband loves and respects his wife and earns her devotion; the result is the continual, mutual respect that builds an effective, strong marriage relationship.

The key to building a healthy marriage is this: Love is action, and it is reciprocal!

The husband loves and the wife responds with respect and honor and so conversely. When things are not going well, the wife should and must still respect him (unless there is abuse), as with the husband who must still love, regardless of how the other is being with you. Only then will your marriage vastly improve! You will be more happy and content! Is this your mindset? *No, I will not respect him; he is a jerk; no, I won't love her, she is a pain.* With this mindset, your marriage is destined to fail! You will be miserable and fall into dysfunction and strife casting a dark shadow for generations to come if you have kids! Do not let pride ruin your's and your family's life and legacy!

How do we do this?

The Ephesians passage starts off telling us to be *imitators of God* or *Follow God's example*. For us to be imitators, we have to know God and His precepts for us, and we do this through reading the Word and following our Lord's example, putting them into practice with our faith. This means we imitate and play forward His love and character in our relationships, especially with our spouses. So, in our relationships, we become *imitators* of God by walking in His love and allowing it to flow in and out so it spills upon others, especially our loved ones. We do this because we honor and reverence our Lord Jesus Christ (Ephesians 5:1-2)!

If you have trouble with the word 'submission,' understand that it is respect and appreciation, not being 'lorded over.' It is love in action, not abuse. And, submission is not to exceed the parameters of the will of God or of love or the Fruit of the Spirit or righteousness. Submission in the Lord is always positive; there can be no room for anything negative. We all submit, to employers, to government, to the elders and so forth. If there is a whiff of negativity, sin, and/or evil in a life of submission, be assured this not by God's hand as this is NOT the submission we are called to in Him.

Wives are not second class participant in the deal; submission in the Lord is not an admittance of unworthiness in the eyes of other humans. Such submission is the acknowledgement that we are undeserving of God's favor, and we are grateful for His blessing and grace. In this, women submit to their husbands for the sake of the love of

Christ and for the Glory of God; they are to be lifted up and cherished and adored. Any other reaction from man is not in keeping with the Lord.

To prove this, submission is not an excuse to batter or put wives down in any way. The directive to husbands is even more daunting than what has been given to the wives! Husbands are called to *love*, which is much greater in importance and prominence than submission! Love is what sets the tone and standard for the relationship. Submission is also a response! Because the husband is loving, because the husband is caring, because the husband is putting his wife's best interests forward, the wife submits, and he earns her devotion and validation. It is the husband's responsibility to set the tone of love and care! The mandate to love, is the leadership role that commands the husband to thoroughly exhibit all of the qualities of biblical character in his relationship with his wife (1 Corinthians 13:4-7).

Key marriage tip: Allow individuality, do not be so pushy on your personal, non-important preferences, like hair styles, dress, music, movies, and TV; just work on being appropriate and presentable and honoring each other's time. Negotiate the differences and remember respect.

In Colossians, we are given a radical call on how to mold a great marriage. The wife's respect is a response to the husband's love for her and his providing of love, safety, security, as well as for having her best interest and care at heart. It is like when we respond to Christ with love, gratitude and service because of His free gift of grace. We do not earn salvation for service;

rather, it is a fruit of our gratitude. It is not to be forced, but offered freely in response to love. It is something we replicate as in responding in kindness so our response to each other is fueling the other's response, and so forth. In this way, we will be escalating love and kindness instead of repression and dysfunction (Colossians 3:18-4:1).

How do we get to this?

The Bible is clear and the call is effectual. It works and is the best plan ever conceived because it requires both to reciprocate God's call and love.

- What are the wives to do? Be tender and kind to your husbands and, most of all, respecting them.
- What are the husbands to do? Earn your wife's respect with unconditional love for her as this is a reflection of what Christ has done for you.
- Wives and husbands, love each other and do not mistreat each other, as Christ has treated you beyond what you deserve or need.

Then God calls the children, to participate in the love of a home by obeying their parents and respecting them, for your obedience is pleasing to our Lord.

This will create a more content home that glorifies the Lord. When we do not do this, we sink into dysfunction and hurt and then destruction. This will also help you live well and right and not be discouraged or lose hope.

In fact, God calls all in the Christian home, servants and workers, to cheerfully work hard, be obedient, and willingly respect your employers both when they are there and when they are not there. The family, as employers, must never mistreat servants and workers. Most people do not have servants anymore, but many have grandparents, nannies, various relatives, grown children and friends living in the home. So, these principles apply today. These actions show respect for our Lord, because when we work for others, we also are working for Christ.

Key marriage tip: See your marriage as a legacy, especially with children. So your godliness and character is played forward and multiplies by family, friends and all that observes you. Be to God's Glory in all you do!

What we put into our homes and work will be paid back to us just as when we mistreat or manipulate, those actions will come back to us too. God has no favorites and will not allow us to get away with evil and wrongdoing. Those who employ people must treat them with respect, pay them an honorable wage, and provide for them in abundance beyond what is due, for this is what our Lord does for us. We all have but one Master and that is Jesus Christ. He is LORD!

Jesus did not give up on us when things went from bad to worse; His grace, forgiveness, and perseverance came through. It is the model relationship for the home, for the love of children, the fellowships and relationships we are to have. The church is the bride of Christ, and He loves her. Your spouse, or intended spouse, is your bride or groom where righteousness, love, commitment, and holiness are to be practiced and exercised in the best and fullest way possible for you (Revelation 21:1-2)!

Key marriage tip: Real respect and love are essential; we are called to right submission! Christ and the church are the prime models for us in a lifelong commitment of monogamous marriage.

Remember, if you want a great Christian marriage get this: There is nothing more important to a man than to feel respected and appreciated. There is nothing more important to a woman than to feel loved and cherished! Get this, and you get a good marriage!

Questions to challenge, inspire and equip you to be better in your commitment, love and marriage:

Read Ephesians 4:29-32; 5:1-33; Colossians 3:18-19; 1 Peter 3:8-9; 5:6-7

1. When you first got married, what did you think was the primary purpose of marriage? Why is it not to please ourselves?
2. What can you do to be better imitators of Christ? How would that improve your marriage? How is real Love reciprocal? How can you practice that?
3. For the husband, how can you better commit and practice real true love and cherish your wife that God gave you? How do you do this when they push your buttons?

4. For the wife, how can you really and truly respect and honor your husband that God gave you? How do you do this when they push your buttons?
5. How do you feel that God wants you to be joyful, happy, and content? How can you be so? How does being focused on Him and not on your circumstances help?

Keep spending time in prayer and commit to pray for your spouse when you first wake up, when you go to bed and throughout the day! Now, also see if you can pray with your spouse, too—at least 5 minutes a day to start. If they are not open to it, do not push it, just pray for it.

CHAPTER 10

Building Marriage Relationship Skills

Do not repay anyone evil for evil. Be careful to do what is right in the eyes of everybody. If it is possible, as far as it depends on you, live at peace with everyone. Romans 12:17-18

First, let's define what communication is about.

From the precepts in the Bible, it is one of the most important skills in life and relationships and essential in marriage. Effective communication is what builds relationships. It is being willing to convey our honest thoughts, attitudes, feelings, and actions to the people in our life in a kind and active listening manner. And as a Christian and in the Christian home, these must be in the parameters that reflects and glorifies Christ. This is the foundation of a successful marriage as well as a healthy church and an affirmative friendship. Without communication, a marriage or any relationship in the church, the workplace, or anywhere can never effectively function.

(Proverbs 29:20; Matthew 21:22; Luke 8:18; Romans 12:10; Ephesians 4:15, 25-29; Colossians 3:5,16, 4:6; 1 Timothy 4:12; James 1:19; 1 Peter 3).

As we grow in our faith and maturity, we will desire Christ as LORD over the ways of the world. If we think we can do what we want while claiming Christ as Lord, we delude ourselves. How can we honor our Lord when we do not honor what He has taught us? Why would we do this with the LORD, who loves and gives us grace? We have to remember that love and respect, even submission, are timeless and effectual biblical precepts are not meant to bring us down or lord it over us as a tyrannical dictator; rather, it is His love in action. God knows what is best, what works, and what creates good and lasting relationships. So, we should strive to live as *imitators* in all we do (John 14:15)!

Key marriage tip: The Christian home is a prime target for Satan and his minions. Be aware and keep in mutual prayer so you are stronger than he.

As we have been discussing here, the prime key to building a healthy marriage is this—love is reciprocal! The husband loves and thus, the wife responds with respect and honor and so conversely—in the midst of their relationship with Christ as LORD! Christ and the church are the prime models for us in a lifelong commitment of monogamous marriage. Let's explore some tried and true practical ways to make this happen.

Here are some simple tips from Scripture to put goodness in action by just watching how you use your attitude and words.

But the fruit of the Spirit is love, joy, peace, forbearance, kindness, goodness, faithfulness, gentleness and self-control. Against such things there is no law. Galatians 5:22-23

- Always place Christ first and foremost in your life, and He will provide and guide (Matthew 6:33).
- Always focus on building your faith and maturity first (Matthew 7:3-5).

- Always pursue love even in toil as the mark of a true follower of Jesus Christ (1 Corinthians 13)!
- Always grasp on grace and how Christ loves you and your spouse, so you can give grace to them (Galatians 2:20-21)
- Always pray together daily (Psalm 127:1; Matthew 18:19).
- Always respect and love your spouse (Ephesians 5:1-2)!
- Always be encouraging, listening, supporting, accepting, trusting, and respecting with love (**Ephesians 4:2**).
- Always express your love to your spouse daily with a good attitude with, words, deeds, and kind touches (**Solomon 8:6-7**).
- Always forgive mistakes and practice forgiveness (Colossians 3:13).
- Never be arrogant, criticizing, threatening, nagging, blaming, complaining, punishing, or bribing (2 Timothy 2:22-24).
- Always laugh and have fun together (Proverbs 17:22).
- Always say "I'm sorry" (1 John 3:4-6).
- Always communicate goodness, ask, don't second guess, thank, praise and listen (Romans 12:19)!
- Always put the needs of your spouse ahead of your own (Proverbs 17:9)
- Never trust your heart; you can only trust the Lord (Jeremiah 17:9)!
- Always be supportive of each other (**Ephesians 4:2-3**).
- Never seek to change your spouse, you can only change yourself (Romans 12:17-18).
- Always use words to build up your spouse, not tear him or her down. (Proverbs 25:11).

- Always have enjoyable talks every day (Proverbs 27:6).
- Never be defensive (Matthew 7:1-5).
- Always say "thank you" and "we" (**Proverbs 10:12**).
- Always go on dates, have fun together (Song of Solomon 7:11-12).
- Never absolutely never give egotism, sarcasm or cynicism (Proverbs 17:4).
- Never speak from anger (Ephesians 4:26).
- Never ever threaten the relationship (Mark 1:15).
- Always Give your spouse at least one compliment every day (Philippians 1:3-6).
- Never take your marriage for granted (Colossians 3:23).
- Always serve one another in love (Galatians 5:13).
- Never talk badly about your spouse to others (James 1:19).
- Always look for solutions, not problems (Proverbs 29:20).
- Always do all the important things together (**Philippians 4:13**).
- Always seek unbiased godly counsel (Psalm 37:30).
- Always discuss outside friendships (like work relationships), never harbor secrets (**Galatians 5:13**).
- Always agree to disagree, you will never agree on everything (**1 John 3:18**).
- Never try to control your spouse (**Philippians 2:2**).
- Never threaten splitting, leaving or divorce (**1 Peter 1:22**).
- Always, in all you do, seek and glorify the Lord (**1 Chronicles 16:11**).

Seek yourself, and you will be sad and lonely in so many ways! Seek Christ and you will be fulfilled and content!

Remember that the heart of any healthy relationship is love and respect!

Key marriage tip: Try new things, go to different restaurant, different vacation destinations, wear different clothes, serve in your church or community together to keep things fresh and exciting. Your goal, in trying new things you learn new things about each other.

When we are not communicating, we will not build a solid, deep relationship. We must be able to ask questions, listen, and be vulnerable to reflect, give disputes in love, and address each other's shortcomings, faults, and areas that need growth. Take it slow and develop your friendship with your spouse first. If you do not do this, then you will be among the countless relationships in our culture filled with miscommunication, hurt, and misery!

Tips for Husbands: If your wife does not respect you, you need to earn it and be patient. Some women will not voice their hearts, so you must discover what it is important and work on the following:

- Women need to feel loved, cherished, safe and protected.
- Listen to her and seek to deeply understand her, let her know you are glad that she is your wife.
- Discuss your feelings. Yes, it is hard, but it is necessary to share your hopes, fears, and dreams.
- Let her know that she is the most precious and the special person to you.

- Be romantic with non-sexual ways, special dates, and simple kind gifts like a flower with a note in her car.
- Find out what it is what makes your wife happy and do it, even if you do not, like hiking.
- Turn away from lustful images!
- Step up; take the role of leadership without condescending or lording over.

Key marriage tip: Marriages thrive when we both have the willingness to work together to commune and solve problems.

The only way your spouse, your friends, relationships at work, acquaintances, or anyone, can know what you feel, need, want, desire, or think, is by you telling them. If you want to be heard, you have to be willing to listen. You have to be willing to put your share of the relationship out on the table first, rather than wait for the other person. Good communication in love with kindness is a must—essential to the understanding of one another.

Tips for Wives: Even if your husband does not seem to cherish you or say what is important to him, you can help turn him on to you with the following:

- Express real lovingly respect and admiration, even if he does not deserve it; he may step up to it.
- Men tend to be prideful; do not keep pointing out past mistakes. Allow him to lead without saying, "I told you so." If he is wrong, respectfully suggest an alternative solution.

- Take notice of the good that he does and show your appreciation for the things he does right.
- Be more enthusiastic about sex and allure him, men like to be admired and pursued too.
- Find out what it is what makes your husband happy and do it, even if you do not share the same interests.
- Be patient; do not have unrealistic expectations!

In all you do in marriage and in life, remember the Fruit of the Spirit will build any relationship and church (Galatians 5:22-23; Colossians 3:12-14).

Remember that LISTENING IS ESSENTIAL! Good friend-makers are good listeners and your spouse should be your best friend. Be the person who listens (John 8:47; James 1:19-25)!

Key marriage tip: Assumptions make the good sitcom plotlines; they do not make good marriages!

What we have been talking about may seem difficult, and perhaps even overwhelming, but take this to heart: *God does not call you to do anything that He has not empowered and enabled you to do!* The cross is the proof of how far He will go for you!

Questions to challenge, inspire and equip you to be better in your commitment, love and marriage:

Read **Mark 12:30-31;** John, chaps 14-15; Galatians 5:22-23; Ephesians 4:29-32; 5:31-33

Look over each of these tips, perhaps take one a day, read the passage and ask yourself and your spouse:

1. How do I exhibit this "Never" trait?
2. How do I exhibit this "Always" trait?
3. What can I do to develop a better willingness to be better at "Always"?
4. What blocks the "Always" from working and being exhibited in me?
5. What can I do to not aloe the "Never" to come about from me?
6. How can I make the "Always" function better, stronger, and faster-even in times of uncertainly and stress?

Keep spending time in prayer and commit to pray for your spouse when you first wake up, when you go to bed and throughout the day! Now also see if you can pray with your spouse, too—at least 5 minutes a day to start. If they are not open to it, do not push it, just pray for it.

CHAPTER 11

Building Marriage Communication Skills

Whatever you do, work at it with all your heart, as working for the Lord, not for men. Colossians 3:23

Upgrade your mindsets to goodness!

Our God has rescued you from your sin through the event of the Cross of which we can never fathom. We are not good enough on our own, but He makes us good enough! Many Christian leaders today do not talk about this, yet it is essential. It is essential to know who you are, your spouse and how we can commune better. Why? Our sins have built a chasm that totally cuts us off from a relationship with and salvation in Christ. Sin has wrecked how we are with one another.

In our election and acceptance of Jesus as Savior by faith alone, making Him Lord over all, we freely obligated ourselves to die (get rid of) to our old nature (sin), and be totally reborn (recreated) in the new nature that He offers us. Christ, living out a sinless life in our place and His death on the cross to pay our penalty of sin, not only purchased our redemption, it also allows us to identify with Him in an intimate way.

Key marriage tip: Be in sync! You and your spouse must be on the same page on key theological and moral ideas.

Be on the same wavelength! For example, if you are a Catholic and marry a Pentecostal, you will not see the world the same and you will be in conflict. This is one of the reasons why God warned the Israelites not to marry the pagans; when they did, it was disastrous as they were out of sync. If you are very different, you must respect and dialog with each other and come to agreement on the majors like the Sovereignty of God and on the minors like speaking in tongues. Work on your sync with each other and honor God's Word and commitment to Jesus Christ as the Great I AM, The Rock, as IS the final arbiter. To work on this, have a mentor you both respect. Remember, love does not condescend!

God, Himself, from His immeasurable love, paid our debt and freed us from His wrath. We must ask ourselves:

What now?
What do I do?
How will I live?

Will I do as I see fit (God may let you) *or, do I go His way, the best way?*

Do we allow Christ's love to motivate and control us, or do we go it alone? If we really, truly believe in Him with sincere trust and obedience, then, it will produce a result. We must allow that result of fruit (Galatians 5:22-25) be in us.

Put to death, therefore, whatever belongs to your earthly nature: sexual immorality, impurity, lust, evil desires and greed, which is idolatry. Colossians 3:5

Does love conquer all?

No! It is just not so! If it were, we would have a very low divorce rate, celebrity marriages would be a big success and everyone would be happy. Everyone starts out 'in love'. In fact, I have never seen a marriage take place where the couple was not *in love*, or at least thought they were in love. Yet, most statistics tell us that over 50% of them are divorced within five years!

If love was enough, those marriages would work out; obviously, love is not enough!

Love, by itself, cannot hold two people together. As we discovered in the previous chapters, most people do not know what love is, nor are they able or willing to apply the characteristics of love that is exhibited in the Bible. They follow their wayward hears and not faith and reason. They forget that love will place the interest of the other first, and, they do not. The feelings and ideas of what they think love is taking the place of working on the relationship. So, communication, as well as understanding and the willingness to work together to solve problems, is left out of the relationship.

In reality, there is no *happily-ever-after* or riding off into the sunset together. Relationships require effort to make them work; they just do not happen. The efforts of listening and effective communication. So, our favorite celebrity gossip, movies and the romance novels do not give us proper reality; in fact, they corrupt our perspectives and thinking so take in faulty ideas and expectations. When our reality is in line with God's, and we are following His precepts, then the adventure of the relationship becomes fun, and we can ride off into that sunset. We can enjoy life better. Just know that that sun will rise the next day, and you may still be lost and confused—perhaps, even hurt. The effort you put in will help keep you on the right path of developing the love relationship with the love of your life.

Remember, authentic Christian love is the turning of our backs to self-concerns, and facing forward to our relationships with family, friends, and neighbors. It is the surrender of our will to His. If love does not take us beyond our self-interests, then what we have is lust, and not love!

Key marriage tip: Understand your differences! Celebrate them! Understand that you are two completely different people, different sex, different thinking, different upbringing, and different experiences. Be willing to respect where the other comes from Be mature, be accepting and listen first, speak second.

So, what can I do to build that love? Pay attention to what and how you say things!

Here are some replacement words you can use to create a better marriage environment; this also works at work, school, and church.

Substitute Negative Words	With	Positive Words
"I can't" and "I won't"	With	"I haven't yet."

"I don't know"	With	"I will find out for you."
"If I"	With	"When I."
"That will be a problem"	With	"That's going to be a challenge."
"I will try"	With	"I will do"
"You are…or, I am…a failure"	With	"We are a success because we learned something."

How many more can you think of?

Who is going to harm you if you are eager to do good? But even if you should suffer for what is right, you are blessed. "Do not fear what they fear; do not be frightened." But in your hearts set apart Christ as Lord. 1 Peter 3:13-15

The ups and downs of marriage may get us down, and the arguments, tension, disagreements, gossip, treachery, betrayal, financial disasters, stress, and false accusations may take its toll on us. When life seems to rise up and wage war against us, our character can grow stronger and our relationships can improve. We can become even stronger and more loving—even more content. The choice is ours!

Key marriage tip: Arguing? Have a disagreement? Have a commitment as to how you will respond and remember the Fruit of the Spirit. Do not raise your voice, do not use foul language, especially around kids, it is extremely destructive, and do not escalate it. Do not bring back the past. Do not belittle! Rather commit to a plan to hear each other, listen, work it out or wait when you are both in a place to listen. Have a commitment that it is safe to talk and share one another's feelings. Respect and treat them as God has treated you!

Will my spouse be the perfect mate to fulfill me?

Again, that would be a firm NO! Nothing created can fulfill you completely. As we are filled with imperfections caused by sin, so we cannot have a mindset that is perfect and understanding like that of God, who is without sin. That is why understanding and applying the precepts of God's Word and not the world of feelings are so important!

Look at it this way, when we accepted Christ's gift of grace, we did become complete in Him. But, not as most people think. We become *declared* complete. Thus, in God's eyes, we are pure; but, in reality and practice, our sinful state is still in practice and all too active. We can strive to become more mature, which is an aspect of sanctification, but, nonetheless, we are still imperfect beings. Sin affects all we do, including our mate selection and our relational skills. So, all we do is corrupt, even while trying to fulfill His will to the best of the ability and the gifts He has given us. We are not even made for this world, rather, for the life to come (Isaiah. 44:9-20; 2 Corinthians 1:22; Galatians 5:5; 5:5; Colossians 3:5).

Love is *not* all you need, especially if you do not know what love is!

If all you have is love, and, let's say that it is real, authentic, biblical love, yes, you will be doing well—very well. However, we need to know that you, I, your spouse, most people, even committed Christians, do not operate in all of those precepts all of the time. Thus, we have to know, have a plan on how we are you going to relate to each other all of the time—from the toothpaste and toilet seat, to sleeping together, sharing personal items, friends, relatives, in-laws, pets, cars, career—and, in addition, handling money, and rearing children? You are no longer in the dating and friend scene, where you can go home to do whatever you want. You are two as one, you have responsibilities, and this is good. Change can be very difficult for some, and, if you feel you made the wrong decision, you entered into an entire, additional set of problems, as well. But you can prevail in Christ and make it work. Exiting the relationship (unless there is abuse or abandonment) will only bring more heart-wrenching hurt and lasting dysfunction for generations.

Here are some replacement thoughts to help line up your thinking to God's call.

Do not conform any longer to the pattern of this world, but be transformed by the renewing of your mind. Then you will be able to test and approve what God's will is—His good, pleasing and perfect will. Romans 12:2

Substitute Negative Thoughts	With	Positive Thoughts
I do not feel loved.	With	God loves me and nothing can buffet that. Romans 8:31; 38-39

I give up.	With	I can. Philippians 4:13
I am too weak.	With	The Lord is my strength. Psalm 27:1
I am a failure.	With	God does not abandon me. 2 Corinthians 4:8-9
I am worthless.	With	I have real value because God made me. Psalm 139 13-16
I am confused.	With	God has a plan for me. Jeremiah 29:11
I am afraid.	With	God gives me power, love and no fear. 2 Timothy 1:7
I feel alone.	With	God is with me. Matthew 28:20; Hebrews 13:5
I feel unfulfilled.	With	I can be content. Philippians 4:11
I do not know what to do.	With	God will give me wisdom. James 1:5
I feel judged.	With	I am not condemned. Romans 8:1

Positive thinking has been negatively viewed in Reformed and Evangelical circles due to its abuse by some preachers. This is certainly not advocating a message that positive thinking solves everything or garners "special" blessing. In fact, the above is not *just* positive thinking. It is thinking in the Way of God's true Truth, and it is living in God's Word. This positive thinking is a call from our Lord as we absorb

His Word and set it firmly in our minds so that we break any cycle of negative-thinking and living outside and away from the Lord.

Remember that the heart of any healthy relationship is love and respect!

When we lose sight of our purpose, what God calls us to in life or in marriage, we will fall into a life of despair, not achieving desired fulfillment. When we follow His precepts, we will find the right person, stay on the right path, and experience the ultimate pleasure and fun. The irony about society is that it seeks all these without including God. Because of this, people become disillusioned and angry with God when they do not get what society promises them.

If we just spend a little more time working on our relationship with each other, we will be miles ahead of the game of life and will enjoy a much happier and purposeful life that would please God, making us, and those around us, happier.

Key marriage tip: Be positive—in the Truth. People do not like negative people as it brings them down. So, be positive and affirming with the love of your life!

Another thing you need to do to build a good marriage is to be accountable to someone, perhaps those in a small group. You will grow and change better and faster by having someone who knows you to push, encourage, and challenge you in the right direction and in the Word.

Questions to challenge, inspire, and equip you to be better in your commitment, love and marriage:

Read **Mark 12:30-31;** John chaps14-15; Galatians 5:22-23; Ephesians 4:29-32; 5:1-33

1. How can you use these replacement words and positive thoughts?
2. How will it improve your marriage?

Keep spending time in prayer and commit to pray for your spouse when you first wake up, when you go to bed and throughout the day! Now, also see if you can pray with your spouse, too—at least 5 minutes a day to start. If they are not open to it, do not push it, just pray for it.

CHAPTER 12

Be a Better Communicator

Let your conversation be gracious and attractive so that you will have the right response for everyone. Colossians 4:6

Building marriage communication and relationship skills

What if you decided to build a house for your family? You then decided to hire an architect, contractor, designer, and landscaper and build your dream home. Sounds wonderful, doesn't it? What if you and your spouse did just this, too? Now, each of you hired a different architect, a different contractor, a different designer, and a different landscaper? Then, you did not have any of them talk to one another, just build and do? What kind of dream home would you have? Now, that is a marriage that does not communicate!

Key marriage tip: To talk about it, and listen more, must be the cornerstone of your marriage relationship. *You shall become one…*

At the writing of this book, for the last five plus years, my son, Ryan, has been learning the piano and violin. He started while he still wore diapers. (This is his choice, by the way.) I take him to the lessons. Through the years, I've sat with him at the piano, helped him hold the violin (so it would not become expensive toothpicks), guided him in practice and listened while he played. Even though I never had the desire or inclination to learn about or play the violin or piano, I now know how! While I have always enjoyed music and appreciate those who play, I never considered doing the same. In proximity and support, I have learned; even though I now know how, I still do not play.

This relates to a lot of Christians who know about the Bible, about faith, about the Fruit of the Spirit, or stewardship and so many other essential Christian life topics. We know it. We just don't practice it. (This is based on my experience as a pastor for the last 30 years.) I do not play the violin or piano. Not that I can't, I just do not want to. I would rather listen to people who are better at it and enjoy it. But, in the case of the Word, we all must partake, learn and apply God's most precious precepts to grow and be better for His service!

Do not merely listen to the word, and so deceive yourselves. Do what it says. James 1:22

These are illustrations of how most Christians tend to lead their Christian lives, knowing, but not doing—knowing, but not practicing. This is how many of our marriages work; we know how to communicate, to love, to share, to commune— we just do not do it. Now, not practicing an elective skill is not a big deal in my opinion. But, knowing how to communicate, an essential skill, and choosing not to, as in knowing how to love and keeping it put away, is pretty detrimental. If I choose not to play the violin, life doesn't change much for me. If I choose not communicate (and I know how), life changes. How would that work out for me? How well is that working for you? Do not be the Christian who knows and does not do, especially in the home!

Key marriage tip: When there is a problem or crises, deal with it by using facts, listening and love, as quickly as possible. Do not hide it, do not prolong it. Prolonged conflict does nobody any good. Deal with one problem at a time; do not escalate and throw other stuff in—nothing can be dealt with or resolved.

Tips to be a Better Communicator

(Proverbs 29:20; Matthew 21:22; Luke 8:18; Romans 12:10; Ephesians 4:15, 25-29; Colossians 3:5, 16, 4:6; 1 Timothy 4:12; James 1:19; 1 Peter 3)

Love each other with genuine affection, and take delight in honoring each other. Romans 12:10

- **Be willing to be open and honest**. Be willing to express feelings about the other, and the desires, aspirations, and plans you see for yourself and for your spouse. This will build communication and trust! If you cannot express yourself, get help. Otherwise, it will only escalate from bad to worse. You cannot gain anything by lying or playing games!
- **Be considerate**. Communication, as well as understanding and the willingness to work together to commune and solve problems, must be a cornerstone of your marriage relationship.
- **Courtesy is contagious**! The care we give our spouses is usually more important than the words we say!

- **Show interest** in your spouse; be positive and sensitive. Do this by asking questions, listening to each other fully, and not dominating the conversation. When you see him or her again, remember the important details so you can bring up what was communicated before and ask how it is going, what you can do to help, and so forth.
- **Take responsibility.** Always communicate without blame; always show the love of Christ!
- **Do not guess.** Seek first to understand what your spouse is saying, do not assume, and make sure they feel understood; this inspires openness and trust.
- **Be sincere.** Saying what you mean and meaning what you say is the golden rule to any effective and edifying communication.
- **Do not be overly sensitive.** You are only responsible for what you say and how you treat others, especially your spouse; you are not responsible for what others say to you or how they treat you!
- **Be yourself; be genuine, honest and real.** Do not pretend or be manipulative. Remember, integrity is imperative at all times!
- **Be kind.** When you have disagreements—and you will—explain your position in kindness with rational and reasonable reasons for it. Do not jump to conclusions or be overly emotional or manipulative. Any good position will be open for comments, evaluation, criticism, and the opinions of the one you are called to love.
- **Listen.** Make sure you hear your spouse's position correctly. If you are not sure, are confused, if it does not make sense, or it is incongruent, ask questions for clarification.

- **Compliment** your spouse's ideas, whether you agree or not, and be courteous. When giving a critique, be constructive, positive, true, and respectful.
- **Paraphrase** back what they said for clarity. If you think there is a misunderstanding brewing, ask a question, "May I restate what I am hearing from you?"
- **Be aware of your body language**. Make sure you are not giving off negative signals or have a callous or insensitive tone. Remember, you may be doing this and not even realize it.
- **Use words wisely**. The choice of our words and the tone of them will have dramatic effects as it greatly affects the meaning, interpretation, and distortion of the message. Choose your words and tone carefully through prayer with encouragement in mind! Remember that most people will not attribute the same meaning to the same words! Clarify what and how you say something!
- **Take feedback**. Allow your spouse and others to give you constructive feedback whether it is ideas, suggestions, critiques, or confrontation; incongruent or not, listen and be in prayer about what you can learn and improve about yourself.
- **Do not be defensive**, Being defensive, cynical, condescending, name calling, labeling people, being prideful, and arrogance are listening, communication and relationship killers!
- **Really listen**. Having selective hearing, ignoring important other information and only willing to listen to what you want to hear will seriously hamper your relationships as well as ability to communicate.
- **Do not jump to conclusions** or be judgmental or legalistic! Having assumptions about your spouse

may or may not be true and hinders listening and communication.

- **Be clear.** Not speaking or communicating clearly, or being dishonest so your spouse cannot hear what you say will lead to them forming untrue assumptions to causing serious and detrimental misunderstandings.
- **Do not jump to conclusions!** Do not form your impressions by preconceptions, stereotyping, or generalizing.
- **Be empathetic**; consider how you would feel in their situation. Good listeners will be sensitive and show care by identifying and having compassion for the other person and not be disconnected or detached. Sometimes, it is necessary in professional type relationships to have set some boundaries when interacting with patients or colleagues. However, it is essential to show empathy and care.

Effective communication is paramount in marriage.

We must be willing to convey our honest thoughts, attitudes, feelings, and actions in a kind and active listening manner that reflects and glorifies Christ. This is the foundation of a successful marriage as well as a healthy church and an affirmative friendship.

Key marriage tip: Your spouse is not an enemy, not an obstacle, not a setback, not a competitor, not a 'them;' rather a 'we.' When you are married you are in the 'our' business, not the 'them' or 'me' business. With a 'we' you become a success, with a 'me' and 'them' approach you will wither away.

Without good communication, a marriage or any relationship in life, the church, the workplace, or anywhere can never effectively work.

More communication tips

- Keep in mind that when a person's feelings are hurt, spouse, boss, friend, relative or…, he or she will retaliate, not negotiate!
- Stay calm, do not overreact! Always, always ask for clarification!
- Whether you are a pastor, doctor, lawyer, or a dog catcher, keeping confidences is paramount!
- Always be a learner; seek what you can learn from your spouse, this person, from this situation, and from mistakes made by you or others.
- To effectively listen, we need to give our spouse our full attention. We must be willing to build the skills of empathetic and active listening. To do this, we first need to concentrate on quieting our own thoughts and concerns so we can hear theirs. We all have a natural, internal commentary going; try to shut it off until afterwards. This will help you engage the person and remember what he or she is saying.
- If you want to interact effectively with and/or influence another person, you first need to understand them!
- When talking to someone, develop rapport by demonstrating sincere interest in him or her; focus on him or her as a child of God by investing time. This should be the most important person in the room for you!

- Honor and hear others' thoughts and feelings; express positive feelings and feedback.
- Listen to the words and try to determine the essence of those words. Keep in mind that what you think they are saying is not always what they are really saying, so ask questions so to clarify and gather more information.

Having a problem? Ask, *What can we do to solve this problem together? What are some steps you see that could resolve this issue?* If that does not work, place the issue on what the purpose of the Christian life is about, to worship and glorify Christ. *How can we develop a solution that glorifies our Lord* (Proverbs 19:11; Matthew 18:15-17; Ephesians 4:29)?

Key marriage tip: In good communication, do not assume. You need to verbalize, build trust and rapport, have no secrets, be transparent, be open and honest, and show the Fruit of the Spirit.

Questions to challenge, inspire, and equip you to be better in your commitment, love and marriage:

Think through the steps you need to take to put good Communication into action in a specific instance, such as, *where is positive communication not functioning properly in my Christian walk and what can I do about it?* What good communication skills are lacking in you? What can you do to develop them and put them into practice and build up your marriage?

1. How do I exhibit good Communication with my spouse?
2. What can I do to develop a better willingness to pursue effective Communication?
3. What blocks good Communication skills from working and being exhibited in me?
4. How can I make Communication function better, stronger, and faster-even in times of uncertainly and stress?

Remember that LISTENING IS ESSENTIAL! Good friend-makers are good listeners. Be the person who listens (John 8:47; James 1:19-25)!

Keep spending time in prayer and commit to pray for your spouse when you first wake up, when you go to bed and throughout the day! Now, also see if you can pray with your spouse, too—at least 5 minutes a day to start. If they are not open to it, do not push it, just pray for it.

CHAPTER 13

How to Solve and Prevent Conflict in Marriage

Whatever happens, conduct yourselves in a manner worthy of the gospel of Christ. Then, whether I come and see you or only hear about you in my absence, I will know that you stand firm in one spirit, contending as one man for the faith of the gospel without being frightened in any way by those who oppose you. This is a sign to them that they will be destroyed, but that you will be saved—and that by God. Philippians 1:27-28

Don't allow disappointments to consume you.

The essential tool to help you mange distress and conflict is how you view it. Disappointments can be defined as the collision between our expectations and our experiences, while ignoring the signposts of God's promises. Our expectations will collide with our experiences and then create a wrecked life of self-pity and resentment. Or, it can lead to a triumphant life. The choice is ours; the key is where we look for our hope! This is about our circumstances and how we look at our Lord. This is about how we see adversity; His sovereignty will totally affect how we learn from and deal with adversity.

Key marriage tip: You must understand what God has said and called us to in marriage; read and know *God has called us to live in peace…in order that we might bear fruit* *for God.* Matthew 5:32; 19:9; Romans 7:1-4; 1 Corinthians 7:10-15.

What consumes us and distracts us?

Unanchored stress and disappointments, along with a detachment from looking to God, will prevent us from seeing His signposts of precepts. We cannot just expect God to get us through without any effort on our part. To grow, we have to struggle and work it out. It is the struggle that helps us; it is what builds us and forms us. Without it, there is no growth or real impacting faith, honest character, genuine patience, or maturity—and thus, unhealthy relationships.

We can grow beyond our natural tendency to put others down by focusing on what Christ did for us and realizing He did that for others too, even the one(s) we seek to *put down.*

The antidote to criticism and bickering is the continual practice of encouragement.

When we decide to bring comfort and consolation to others, rather than condescending comments, complaints and retorts, we are actually putting courage into another person. Consider that when we put down a friend, a loved one, or a spouse, we are actually saying *you are not worthy, you are not loved, and you are not accepted or appreciated.* We are actually called to build up our friends, coworkers, and spouse. We are called to make them feel loved, accepted, and appreciated. We are to show Christ's love, not our disapproval.

The Bible gives us clear direction on how we are to keep our attitude and mouths under God's direction, not ours. Proverbs gives us many verses that shows us our human weaknesses and fallen state that seeks out the destruction of one another instead of building one another up as God desires us to do.

Start to consciously and conscientiously replace your negative feedback with positive comments. Start to use complements and be encouraging without faking it.

Starting a quarrel is like breaching a dam; so drop the Matthewer before a dispute breaks out. Proverbs 17:14

What can you do?

Pay attention to yourself and how your spouse reacts to you. When we are focused on seeing the failings, disappointments, corruption, and deceit in others, especially the one you are wedded to, usually it is because we are filled with it ourselves, and we do not take the Word of God seriously. What if God judged us as we do others? So, the answer is, *don't!*

Key marriage tip: Honor each other as who they are. Work on yourself to be a better you, the you God made you to be. Quality change is contagious!

Don't play these games. Your marriage and relationships are too precious and valuable to destroy them with our whims or hurts. Yet, Christians can be some of the most critical and arrogant people on earth! As Christians, we need to be an example for Him wherever we are, set ourselves above pettiness, and let God remove our pride!

Remember that the heart of any healthy relationship is love and respect!

Essential Points to Remember:

For out of the heart come evil thoughts, murder, adultery, sexual immorality, theft, false testimony, slander. Matthew 15:19

1. **You are Christ's loved one (2 Corinthians 12:9-10):** So is your spouse! Do not take the problem as a personal attack, even if it is. You may be a part of the conflict, or a third party trying to resolve it. To get through it, you must realize that you are Christ's child, so is your spouse; He is your identity and defense! When you understand that, you can better see your role as a relationship builder—even when the other person is seeking to tear you down. This first point has saved me a lot of stress and disappointment!

2. **Conflict is an Opportunity** (1 Corinthians 6:1-8): It is an opportunity to learn and give God honor. It is not necessarily bad or the end of a relationship. Know for certain that God can use conflict, whether it is sin, bad choices, a wrong turn, or a misunderstanding, and transform it into good if you let Him. It will make your marriage stronger if handled right. God will be glorified, and you will grow in character, maturity, trust, love, obedience, and in faith.

3. **Listening** (Proverbs 28:13; James 1:19-25; 1 John 1:8-9): The first job is listening, without opening your mouth. Effective listening and getting each party to listen is essential! Until each one listens, nothing

productive will happen. People need to be heard; the one who listens earns the right to be heard and resolve the issue. Make sure they know you are listening by giving eye contact, leaning forward, and being relaxed. Restate to clarify what you heard with as few words as possible, saying, *this is what I heard*...Be open and say, "I'm confused; let me try to restate what I think you said." Or, "You have said so much; let me see if I have heard it all."

4. **Understand Forgiveness** (Psalm 103:12; Isaiah 43:25; 1 Corinthians 13:5; Colossians 3:12-14): Most Christians have a pale sense of the wonder that we have been forgiven, and often fail to show that forgiveness to others when wronged. Forgiveness is absolutely crucial for any relationship to continue, and critical to resolve any conflict! Remember how much you have been forgiven; do not fail to show it to others! Remember, God does not treat us the way we tend to treat others.

5. **Communication** (Luke 15:11-24): Seeking understanding is more important than resolving the issue. Most issues do not need to be resolved if all parties can understand one another's situation. Mediating a marriage dispute? Get them to talk and listen, and you are on the road to recovery! *Why is the person hurt? Why do they feel that way? What do they want? What can be done?*

Applying these points to a marriage problem

But we Christians have no veil over our faces; we can be mirrors that brightly reflect the glory of the Lord. 2 Corinthians 3:18

Each of these points is a biblical way to deal with a marriage dispute through working with a qualified pastor or counselor. The principle issue is reconciliation with a *win/win* scenario. We can do this by realizing who we are in Christ as we previously discussed, and we are to mirror Christ-like character in our marriage even when it is tough! We have to lift the veil that blinds us to love, opportunities, and reconciliation; the veil blinds us to Christ as well!

Key marriage tip: Try to see your spouse as God does, as His child and His provision to you. When we see this, we see Christ and can better honor and cherish them.

It is my experience, in countless marriage counseling sessions, that about 90% of the time a misunderstanding is escalated by the pushing of each other's *buttons*, and by being blinded by the veil of pride and hurt. Both have to be willing to take a step back and work on themselves spiritually in maturity, and commit to not escalate the matter. Also, keep to one issue at a time; do not allow the whole can of worms to be dumped.

Work on one *worm* at a time, one problem or issue at a time!

The steps can be effectively engaged. It will do wonders if a couple can act cordially to each other, if they can sit together, go through these steps one at a time, and spend a lot of time in prayer. But, it usually takes a pastor or counselor to make this process more effective and pleasant.

Each person brings his or her faults into any relationship.

There are no perfect people. We all have personality dysfunctions and shortcomings which we have to be willing to work on. In the next chapter, we will be talking about relationship killers, such as being defensive, which greatly comes into play in resolving disagreements. (For the counselor: Explain these *killers* (see next chapter) to the couple if you are the counselor, to yourself if you are in the argument, and commit in the counseling session at home and not to engage in such destructible practices.) You have to be willing to work on yourself first (Matthew 7:3-5).

A married couple is on the same team; you are not each other's enemy! So, be willing to see your spouse as your teammate, and not your rival. In that way, you can avoid seeing the other as the problem, and focus on the issue and the solution!

Key marriage tip: Chores, responsibilities, house work, yard work and so forth can be daunting and a place of contention. Try to have appropriate responsibilities, so no one person is overburdened. And try to enjoy it, it is your home, make it home sweet home, comfortable and honoring.

Marital research has shown that 80% of problems do not even have to be solved when the couple talks through the issues and reaches mutual understanding (*Focus on the Family*). Most issues can just be talked out when both apply listening, understanding, and the Fruit of the Spirit over their will and hurt. Only the most difficult of problems will involve the use of Matthew 18 and intervention.

Questions to challenge, inspire and equip you to be better in your commitment, love and marriage:

Read **Mark 12:30-31;** John, chaps 14-15

1. Are you grateful for what Christ has done or do you take it for granted?
2. What do you need to do to cement and practice this paramount point to build a healthy marriage, that the heart of any healthy relationship is love and respect?
3. Men need respect, even when they do not deserve it! As a wife how can you do this?
4. Women need to be loved and cared for, even when they do not earn it. As a husband how can you do this?
5. Your marriage is all about grace, that we receive that we must also distill and pass on. How will you do this?

Keep spending time in prayer and commit to pray for your spouse when you first wake up, when you go to bed and throughout the day! Now also see if you can pray with your spouse, too—at least 5 minutes a day to start. If they are not open to it, do not push it, just pray for it.

CHAPTER 14

How Marriage Relationships Breakdown

Where there is strife, there is pride, but wisdom is found in those who take advice. Proverbs 13:10

Remember, we can build a healthy marriage by understanding, preventing, and solving conflicts.

What we are going to do in this chapter is take a look at the mechanics of how relationships tend to break down, stop working, become skewed, and why they give us all those headaches and problems. Knowing how things break down will give us insights on what to do to prevent the breakdown and actually make things stronger. This is how engineers study structures—analyzing why things failed and account for the loads, tensions, and available materials to make a practical and safe design. In marriage, we can examine how we tend to treat others, what we do when we are mistreated, how we react, how we come across to others, how others react to us, how our hurts turn into giving hurt, and so forth. In examining these things, we can be better equipped to do better. And, most importantly, we can better do what Christ calls us to do.

Key marriage tip: The essential working component to keep any relationship functioning is the ability to lower one's pride in order to forgive. To keep a marriage not just functional, but vibrant, we must forgive, and we forgive as Christ has forgiven us—completely.

We have to keep in mind that the call of marriage is about building the relationship on Love and Respect, Cherishing, Honoring and Forgiveness. Releasing hurt, not banking hurt. Know yourself, know your spouse, and keep the commitment to make it work.

Sometimes we force marriage to do something it was not designed to do, and we turn this most intimate and important relationship into a place of loneliness, worry, hurt and strife. We take what was to be good and turn it into a warzone void of the practice of love, mercy, and our growth in maturity, but rather hone our weapons of pride, arrogance, condescension, and contempt, or just withdraw, staying angry and bitter. We model these practices for our children and expect them to have better lives and marriages when all we've really taught them is how *not* to do it.

Key marriage tip: How you handle conflict will determine how your marriage and children will succeed or fail, whether you will have a dysfunctional or a loving home.

The Breakdowns that creates the Breakup

There are five key aspects that are fueled from our pride with which we humans come against each other like animals in our relationships. These symptoms become our arsenal for attacking others so we are protected from their attack. We use them to self-protect by creating offensive measures to protect ourselves while destroying others, encompassing everything from simple arguments to total war. These are the root issues from which our behaviors and responses stem. The five responses are:

1. Being Defensive!
2. Being Critical!
3. Being Condescending!
4. Withdrawing from others!
5. Uncontrolled Anger

These are the rotten fruits from our sinful nature and pride. Be honest and ask yourself:

> *How often do these defense mechanisms take place in your relationships?*

How often have you personally engaged in one or more of these?

Defensiveness, criticism, contempt and or withdraw. These are all formed from our anger, disappointments, and hurt and all rooted in our—pride. This is a cancer in the living body of relationships. In these negative, dysfunctional responses, we will push God aside and fuel them with our anger and betrayal, continuing the cycle of relationship breakdown (1 Peter 3:1-12)!

Defensiveness is a weapon that enables you to be negative to others. It fools you into not taking responsibility. This comes into play in our communication by warding off of a question we do not want to answer or by verbally attacking someone so that we are not attacked first. It permits you to over-explain your position to the detriment of the other person. You will not be able to listen, see the facts, or see your role in the conflict. It is projecting blame on someone else and causes you to be skeptical of others motives and intentions. While the blame is on them, we are ducking out of our responsibility. For more, just read Proverbs, Chapter 17.

Defensiveness is a form of selfishness as the concern is only on us and not the other person. We need to see the other person as a child of God, too! We need to see His love for us and them! Only in seeing others as God sees them (and us), can we grasp the wonders He has for us.

What does Defensiveness look like? Do you have the passion to always defend yourself, to have an excuse for every occasion? Do you always use the phrase "I" or "me" to the point "we" and "us" never come up? Do you have an excuse for every possible occasion? Are you the type of person who rarely apologizes or admits any fault? Do you ward off people's attacks by attacking them first? You may have a problem with defensiveness! Believe it or not; what you have to say is not more important than hearing what they have to say!

Being Critical is the best way to escalate any conflict. This rotten symptom is a weapon that helps create weapons for the other side, too. It builds the "defensiveness" and "withdraw" armaments in the other person. It is a weapon factory that makes weapons for both sides! It creates a negative response that keeps escalating back and forth to one another. It can take a minor disagreement and turn it into a full blown conflict. This weapon will not allow a ceasefire or solution so the circumstances will get worse and worse. It hurts others before they can hurt or continue to hurt you.

What does Being Critical look like? We attack the other person with put-downs, devious remarks, and sayings such as, *you are always*…or, *you never*…mean looks. Maybe we are seeking to be verbally dominant for whatever personal agenda we may have. This is just the escalation of negativity. In a marriage, it can be putting down our spouse or not caring how their day was. It can also be exhibited by always talking about you and never caring or listening to another person. This is being self-centered and not Christ-centered.

A Condescending attitude is a weapon that cancels out the other person's value. It declares that they are not worthy of you, so you treat them with arrogance and put them down. It is a defensive weapon to protect your insecurities by claiming others as insecure or inferior. You put them down before they put you down. This symptom tells you that the thoughts and feelings of the other person are worthless. Deceiving yourself in this way justifies not taking risks. It is usually rooted in low self-esteem and not realizing who you are in Christ. This devalues people!

What does Being Condescending look like? We will we will pass on the hurt and blame with antagonistic and inappropriate humor, mock the person, ridicule their ideas, their things, their clothing, and dismiss anything to take off the attention from you. What does God have to say about our being contemptuous? It is not good! In Romans 2:1-16, we are told that those who judge others, and disobey God themselves, are inexcusable, and will not escape the judgment of God. Being judgmental will not work; it will only backfire on you.

Withdrawal is a form of avoidance. This is the unwillingness to solve issues and or explain your feelings. It is not giving up; rather it is a first strike weapon that prevents and disrupts communication. We do this by not listening, not caring, getting up and leaving the person. It is a way to not participate so you can "turn off" yourself during a disagreement.

What does Withdrawal look like? The person may just feel overwhelmed and shut down; they stop listening, stop responding, and/or stonewall. The mindset is: If I do not engage, there is no conflict. Unfortunately, the exact opposite occurs; by "ignoring" the other person, you escalate whatever conflict is present.

How can I bridle these cancerous emotions and attacks?

Finally, all of you, be like-minded, be sympathetic, love one another, be compassionate and humble. Do not repay evil with evil or insult with insult. On the contrary, repay evil with blessing, because to this you were called so that you may inherit a blessing. For, "Whoever would love life and see good days must keep their tongue from evil and their lips from deceitful speech. 1 Peter 3:8-10

When we become aware of these cancerous underpinnings that we all harbor, we can then start to bridle them. In this way, they can be controlled and steered away from the harming of our loved ones and friends.

How do you stop this? By really understanding and knowing who you are in Christ and by the knowledge that God accepts you in spite of your failures and sin because of His delivered grace for us. This realization helps us in all aspects of relationship building, so we can choose to be deliverers of His grace to others. By being willing to stop the escalation of relationship breakdown through the exchange of our hurt and anger for love, grace, and forgiveness, our lives will be tremendously more content, joyful, and fulfilling.

So, what can I do to stop these defense mechanisms—pride and self-centeredness—from ruining my relationships?

- Start to be aware of how you come across to others.
- Listen to positive feedback as well as the negative.
- Ask a friend or pastor for advice, and be willing to listen without engaging in negative attitudes.

Realizing that you are engaging in disruptive behaviors is half the battle; the other half is much easier.

Key marriage tip: Beware that escalation will only harm yourself and your spouse and family. Rather, if you start to engage in these dysfunctions, calm down, walk away, and look to solve rather than hurt.

Help from God's Word! First Peter, Chapter 3 gives us a passionate precept—the will of God on how we are to treat one another in marriage and solve conflict. This is a call to work within the boundaries of culture with the Fruit and Call from God. Here, Peter is actually reminding his congregation to show love as if they have forgotten what Christ and the Fruit of the Spirit are all about. We must use this passage as a template, a Christian living checkup of how we are to treat others and see if we are healthy in Christ and in showing the work that He did in us (John 17:20-23; Romans 12:9-21).

The bottom line to make our homes happy and not dysfunctional is to be considerate in all that we do to whomever is in our life. This passage also echoes what James told us in Chapter Four (1 Peter 3: 1-12).

Lasting marriages have two important ingredients: A style of resolving conflict that avoids the five diseases and a large dose of positive interactions that overrides negative interactions by five to one.

Questions to challenge, inspire and equip you to be better in your commitment, love and marriage:

Read **Mark 12:30-31;** John, chaps 14-15; Ephesians 4:29-32; 5:1-33; 1 Peter 3: 1-12

1. How can you be Christ's diplomat when you have disagreements and setbacks?
2. How are these passages a template, a Christian living?
3. How can 1 Peter 3: 1-12 be your check-up on how we are to treat others?
4. What can you do to work within the boundaries of your culture with the Fruit and Call from God to be more considerate? What would this look like? Can you think of a specific instance of this?
5. Do you think a deeper connection develops when we are considerate? Have you experienced this? What can you do to make this happen more?

It is the glory of God to conceal a matter; to search out a matter is the glory of kings. Proverbs 25:2

Defense mechanisms are Gleaned from Dr. John Gottman's research and lectures at Fuller Seminary and my work at the Schaeffer Institute, and my book, *Book Field Guide to Healthy Relationships.* This research has provided a valuable understanding of why marriages succeed and fail. Dr. Gottman's books and Dr. Richard Krejcir's Book, *The Field Guide to Healthy Relationships* can help couples use these new insights to improve their marriage. However, sometimes self-help advice is not enough to keep a marriage from sliding down the slippery slope toward divorce. Marriage counseling would be a logical next step; do not forget to use the resources of your church or a good counseling service.

CHAPTER 15

When Marriage Goes Awry

Finally, all of you, be like-minded, be sympathetic, love one another, be compassionate and humble. Do not repay evil with evil or insult with insult. On the contrary, repay evil with blessing, because to this you were called so that you may inherit a blessing. For, "Whoever would love life and see good days must keep their tongue from evil and their lips from deceitful speech. They must turn from evil and do good; they must seek peace and pursue it. For the eyes of the Lord are on the righteous and his ears are attentive to their prayer, but the face of the Lord is against those who do evil. 1 Peter 3: 8-12

God wants us to treat our spouse with the utmost empathy, care, and self-control.

Consider that the application to husbands is to show more consideration. This is not because of mental, spiritual, moral weakness, or inferiority, or that one is better than the other; rather, it is because God has placed, in the order of creation, the husband as head of the home, just as Christ is the head of the church. Men and women have different roles, yet each one is equal in the sight of God! Thus, when the husband loves and respects his wife and earns her devotion, the result is the continual, mutual respect that builds an effective, strong marriage relationship.

Key marriage tip: Control your pride! If you do this, you will be on the winning side of faith, life and harmony!

Look at it this way, in the context of this First Peter passage, it says, *as heirs,* meaning the fellowshipping together in Christ. This is referring to both husband and wife receiving the beneficiary love from Christ, equal in His sight and purpose, but with different roles. We show respect to our spouse because Christ has died for her just as He has for the husband (Galatians 3:28)!

Key marriage tip: There is a connection to how we treat our spouse that goes deeper than we realize between how we treat others and how God responds to us, especially in a family situation.

If you need a baseball bat to the head to get this, God gives us one. He tells us that if we mistreat our spouse, especially for the husband whose call is to love, He *hinders our prayers!* Meaning, if you can't get this, God does not want to hear from you—just like a parent does to a disobedient child (1 Peter 3: 7)!

If the husband fails to show consideration, he jeopardizes his own spiritual formation. When we refuse to follow God's clearly revealed will or are estranged from others, we become estranged in our relationship with God, thus cutting ourselves off from God's blessings and power. Remember, we are in relationship to Christ through the Church that then flows from the husband to the wife and children (Matthew 5:23-24; Romans 8:14-17; Ephesians 5:23-24; 1 Timothy 3:14-15; 5:1-2; 1 Peter 1:14-17).

Treating a wife by cherishing her was a radical precept in the first century! When women were basically possessions, marriage contracts would advocate that the husband forces his wife to submit with absolute obedience. They could throw out unwanted babies and, in the lower classes, make life miserable for them. In the higher class, there was more social pressure and liberation for women. Some of the philosophers stated since women are physically weaker (this was desirable for cohabitation), and Jewish theologians stated that they were also morally weaker, using Eve as the example.

However, Scripture does not uphold this! Peter and Paul emphasized a very radical idea to the churches and readers when they instructed them to love, and because of love to submit. To Paul, love was a duty (1 Corinthians 13). It was even considered weak by the *macho* mindsets of the times as well as with many people today. But, it is not weak; it is building the strength of a relationship and the bond of a family by creating a mutual partnership!

When things go awry, the plan is: *Do Not Repay!*

Do not repay, is a call, a precept as in this is God's will for us, to not seek revenge or to retaliate against those who have wronged us, especially friends and family. Yes, this does not apply to those who wage war or to police intervention, rather to harmony in the home (Proverbs 20:22; Romans 12:17; 1 Peter 3: 7-12).

Peter, in Chapter Three of his first Epistle, is perhaps, directly quoting Jesus in this passage. Where we are called to bless and do good to those who do not like us or who When we pay someone back to get even, we only end up escalating the issue and thus hurting ourselves and usurping God's authority to judge. Rather, we are told to have *harmony* and be *sympathetic* (1 Corinthians 4:12; 6:12; 6:18; Ephesians 5:8-10; 1 Thessalonians 4:1-2; 5:12-15).

What this is about, we are told not to retaliate, as the next key word in the passages tells us, do not engage an *insult with insult*. As in, do not take your hurts and turn them into weapons of hurt upon others, so we do no escalate or make the situation worse. This does not mean we are to endure abuse or unlawful actions; rather, it has to do with our attitude. It is a balance between the exercise of the Fruit of the Spirit and setting up boundaries to protect us (Proverbs 16:32; 25:28; Romans 13:11-14; Galatians 5:22-23; Tim. 2:22, Hebrews 12:2; 13:4; 2 Peter 1:5-7).

By the way, did you know that nowhere in the Old Testament does it say to hate your enemies? It just tells us not to be like them. Some have used Psalm 139:19-22 as an excuse; however, in context, the request is clearly for those who are wicked. Proverbs 25:21-22 tells us that when we overcome evil with good, it totally disorientates those who hurt us, sending them into chaos and confusion, until they are convicted or fall deeper into sin and death.

This should give you a wake up call that this is the best revenge; let their own misdeeds haunt them, and let the perfect Judge deal with them! This is how we solve a marriage crisis, stop the button pushing and the escalation, and calm down; when you are ready to talk, listen and do not use your defensive mechanisms. That way, we can understand and identify with another, putting ourselves in their shoes so we can have real compassion. Scripture tells us when we show peace in all situations, then we will see how your family will vastly improve (Exodus 23:4-5; Leviticus 19:17-18; Proverbs 25:21-22).

So what do we do when things go awry?

What can I do? God calls us to bear one another's burdens without letting those burdens break us.

How do I do this? By understanding the role of restoring, we can pursue restoration and not the defensiveness of our hurts. We have the tendency to protect our hurts, fears, and wounds from others by attacking them first. In military terms, this is a classic preemptive attack, which is the *attack-before-they-attack-us* approach. However, in relationships, we are not to be at war in a combative mode; rather, we are to be in a reconciling mode.

Start to consciously replace your negative feedback with positive comments. Start to use complements and be encouraging without faking it. See yourself as a diplomat of Christ and conform your attitude likewise. See others as Christ sees them—as His child and loved by Him. When you have a concern or a conflict, slow down, observe your attitude and behaviors, and start to listen to the other person. Repeat what they said and give them positive feedback. Seek the effective repair of your relationship and not the escalation of the hurt or anger. Deal with the concern in a loving way. Place the focus on the situation and not the person, validating them as a person for whom you care while seeking forgiveness and reconciliation. (See the "replacement words" in **Chapter V,** *Understanding the Importance of Being Good of my Book Field Guide to Healthy Relationships.*)

Consider how you use personal pronouns such as *"you" i.e. you never, you always, you should, you cannot...*

A simple replacement of "you" with "I" and "we" will do wonders to your relationships. Such as, I *would, I like, I love, I feel, I hear, how might I*...And, *we should, we can, we could, we need, in what ways might we...*

By taking the "you" away you place "yourself" into the conversation.

Taking the "you" out brings you in! You will be able to remove blame so the focus is about reconciliation. You will be able to remove contempt, because you have to bend your pride, to show forgiveness to the other person. You will be able to remove the criticism, as you cannot criticize with an "I". You will then be able to remove defensiveness, because the wall made of the bricks of "You" has been torn down. You can be a builder and equipper not a person who pushes away others!

Who can discern his errors? Forgive my hidden faults. Keep your servant also from willful sins; may they not rule over me. Then will I be blameless, innocent of great transgression. Psalm 19:12-13

Key marriage tip: The solution to strife is to stay away from judgments, seeking fault in others, avoiding put-downs, and focusing on goodness.

We already all have way too much criticism in our lives from our coworkers, boss, teachers, parents, siblings, friends, the media, and church members; there is no need to add to it. We will be able to praise, encourage and respect our spouse and the people around us while earning their trust because we made them safe and secure.

Be Respectful!

We can be better at building our communication and solving conflict through being *respectful.* When we are being:

Responsible—we are **e**volving our relationship, becoming more...
  Sincere, learning...
  Patience, finding...
  Enjoyment,
  Contentment, and building...
  Tenderness,
  Faithfulness,
  Understanding, and...
  Listening skills:

Respectful! We can build this security by speaking the truth in love, encouragement and listening. When we do not put a stop to our avoidances and put-downs of others, this will boomerang back at us. Remember, relationships are communal and continual.

The bottom line to stop relationship dysfunction is to know we do not need to always be defending and attacking others, whether it is a legitimate betrayal from a trusted friend or spouse or a misunderstanding. Why? Our true security is in Christ; when we realize this, we can put up with the dysfunction and the negativity of others, and reduce our fear so we can pursue relationships and their healing.

More practical helps

First of all, *stop it, stop it, stop it,* as the great pseudo psychologist, Dr. Bob Hartley from the American TV show from the 70's *The Bob Newhart Show*, which is great wisdom not just comedic entertainment.

So, how do I stop it?

- **First, Calm Down!** Take a deep breath, then a rest, walk away if necessary, for at least twenty minutes, so the emotions subside and the conflict does not spiral out of control.
- **Second, PRAY!** We can't pray effectively when upset, so take a breather first. Allow God to reset you and your temperament.
- **Third, Think it Through!** What are you doing? What is the game plan? What will happen in this course of events? What will this do to your family, health. Now commit to being positive and not negative with your thoughts, feeling and words.
- **Forth, LISTEN!** Hear them out! Change your attitude toward God and His call and precepts, and treat your

spouse with love and respect, even when they do not deceive it.

- **Fifth, Now you can talk with each other, and Speak Non-defensively!**
- **Sixth, Validation.** Tell them, with empathy and understanding, they are important and loved, you care and are here for them!

  - **Don't assume** (you know what your partner is saying or that they understand what *you're* trying to communicate)
  - **Be concrete** (in what you say). Say what you want, what you need. But remember not to blame or label the other. This allows for communication of difficult feelings.
  - **Example**—*Not* "You never listen to me. You're impossible, terrible, etc." *But* (Being concrete] "I need to feel more heard." (Not assuming) "Something is blocking us from hearing each other."

Remember the relationship killers:

1. Being Defensive!
2. Being Critical!
3. Being Condescending!
4. Withdrawing from others!
5. Uncontrolled Anger

Do I always have to do this? What about if the other person is pushing too much?

Do not jump to conclusions! Do not form your impressions by preconceptions, stereotyping, or generalizing.

What about abuse? If you are in an abusive relationship, get out of it, even if it is a marriage. Abuse is physical, mental and spiritual. It is hitting, manipulating and the refusal to stop and get help. Get out and get help. IF the abuse completely stops and will not reoccur, reconciliation is possible. Make sure you have a trusted and trained counselor helping you in the process! Keep in mind the precepts we discussed in Chapter XI "How to set Boundaries." *in my Book Field Guide to Healthy Relationships.*

Key marriage tip: Do not threaten or intimidate or use foul language; your spouse is supposed to be your best friend. There is no place for foul langue in the home; patience, wisdom, tact and kind wit overrule vulgarity!

Key marriage tip: Do not become obsessed with winning; rather, be obsessed with real love and faith. We do not need to shock our loved ones; we need to point to the Love of Christ!

The bottom line in stopping relationship dysfunction is to know we do not need to always be defending and attacking others, whether it is a legitimate betrayal from a trusted friend or spouse or a misunderstanding. Why? Our true security is in Christ; when we realize this, we can put up with the dysfunction and the negativity of others, and reduce our fear so we can pursue relationships and their healing.

Remember Christ did not give up on us when things went from bad to worse with our sin. His grace, forgiveness, and perseverance came to us anyway!

Questions to challenge, inspire and equip you to be better in your commitment, love and marriage:

Read **Mark 12:30-31**; John, chaps 14-15; Ephesians 4:29-32; 5:1-33; 1 Peter 3: 1-12

1. How would you define unconditional love? Have you ever felt or experienced it? Have you ever given it?
2. How do you feel that Christ has treated you beyond what you deserved or needed? How does this help you with the attitude of love, respect and submission?
3. What can you do to not jump to conclusions or preconceptions, stereotyping, or generalizing?
4. What about that Jesus will not allow us to get away with evil and wrongdoing? Now, what are you going to do about loving and respecting your spouse? Need ideas? Read 1 Corinthians 13 and one day at a time practice one of the aspects of love toward them, whether they deserve it or not!

Having a problem? Ask, *what can we do to solve this problem together? What are some steps you see that could resolve this issue?*

If that does not work, place the issue on what the purpose of the Christian life is about—to worship and glorify Christ. *How can we develop a solution that glorifies our Lord* (Proverbs 19:11; Matthew 18:15-17; Ephesians 4:29)?

Remember that LISTENING IS ESSENTIAL! Good friend-makers are good listeners. Be the person who listens (John 8:47; James 1:19-25)!

CHAPTER 16

Forgiveness

Then Peter came to Jesus and asked, "LORD, how many times shall I forgive my brother when he sins against me? Up to seven times?" Jesus answered, "I tell you, not seven times, but seventy-seven times. Matthew 18:21-22

God gives us a call of forgiveness.

Allow me to make this clear up front: If you know your Word, you should know that there is nothing more important or effectual in our Christian life than forgiveness—period! Forgiveness is the essential core of the Gospel and the essential component to making life work. Life as Christians is centered upon Christ's forgiveness for our sins and our ability to play it forward and forgive others who trespass against us.

Key marriage tip: Real effective forgiveness takes work and time! It flows from a heart that is redeemed and satisfied by the Blood of the Lamb.

Forgiveness will always be easy when we are the one who needs it; yet, it is so hard when we need to give it. Even though forgiveness can be so difficult, we absolutely can <u>and</u> must forgive. This is the essential component to keep any relationship functioning. Forgiveness is the essence of Christianity and marriage. What do we do in those times when we are feeling very unlike Christ? The solution is easy, and the practice can be tough—increase our prayer and decrease our pride. The Holy Spirit empowers us. Jesus intercedes for us and has lived and died and risen all for forgiveness. God has planted within each of us the means to forgive and the amazing grace to help us be forgiven and to forgive. Our responsibility? We must lower our pride in order to forgive. In order to keep and have a vibrant marriage, not merely functional, we must forgive, and we must forgive as Christ has forgiven us—completely.

Key marriage tip: To understand forgiveness, we need to look to Christ, who forgave us when we did not earn or deserve it. We can have mercy upon our spouse and family so to cancel their debts as Christ did with us!

Forgiveness is something <u>extremely special</u> which we are given, as He forgave us, and something precious that we are to replicate and share with others. It is not easy. Sometimes, forgiveness seems nearly impossible. True forgiveness is not impossible, although it requires the practice of maturity, the patience to allow the process to unfold, and the diplomacy to endure it.

What is Forgiving all about? Forgiving someone is essentially the release of a debt. This **comes about by the realization of how much we have been forgiven by Christ, knowing that we deserve none of this. This enables us to forgive the trivial things that are done to us in comparison. Forgiveness** involves not being resentful about the wrongs that we have received. We can heal relationships **by being willing to step beyond our harm and upset and express Christ's love.**

(Psalm 32; Matthew 18:21-35; Luke 23:34; **Ephesians 4:32;** Colossians 3:13**)**

If we refuse to forgive? Well, dark and ugly things will come into our lives. Do any of these sound familiar? Blame, resentment, being judgmental and tolerant (not to be mistaken with being Biblically discerning), pride, envy, jealousy, malice, callous, cynical, and bitter. It is true that even demonic encounters can be present in our lives as these are the dark, light-robbing, rotten fruits of the unforgiving person. When we refuse to repent and forgive, we are concealing ourselves from God and His best for us! Unforgiveness allows bitterness to root and grow so that it festers, and it corrupts our whole being, destroying our marriage and any other relationship. Bitterness becomes our driving force and identity. This true dysfunction produces endless hurt and more dysfunction in our homes and with all whom we meet. Do you understand why it is so important to guard against bitterness? Thank God, He has empowered us and shown us The Example so that we beware unforgiveness and not let it block the flow of the Holy Spirit and the rest of the Fruit of the Spirit—especially self-control and love!

A choice is given: We can have lives free of the burden of unforgivness and truly enjoy what Christ has given, or we can be bitter and live in the darkness of everything opposite faith, hope, and love. We can carry the burden or pass it on to our Lord who graciously and completely will bear!

When we do not forgive, we walk a path of self-destruction brought on by the build up of that resentment and the unfulfilling nature of revenge. There is no disease, no injury, no illness so destructive as unforgiveness. Nothing will wither our soul more than storing up this disease of *unforgiveness*. Pride and arrogance will take you over, control, and ruin you. For our consideration and conviction, just read in Job 5:2, *Resentment kills a fool, and envy slays the simple.*

The goal of forgiveness is allowing Christ to transform us to our full potential.

Most of us will probably go through bad things in life. Even if we don't experience something directly, we know that others do suffer. These are not personal attacks, and the Lord does not wish us harm; rather, the good and bad in life is a strengthening of our character so that we can be better used by our LORD.

Consider this: Love with mercy is the power that builds our home!

The joy and happiness of who we are in Christ will bubble over, not just covering the pain and hurt but removing it! And, remember, forgiveness isn't merely a "good idea" or something to apply in certain situations or for "other people". Forgiveness is a mandate from our LORD.

We can take great comfort in knowing that He is working while we are waiting, and even suffering.

If your spouse is resentful and not responding to your efforts, you can press on, knowing Christ is still at work. We can best practice forgiveness by realizing how much we have been forgiven. We can be imitators of that forgiveness bought by blood of Christ when others willfully or unknowingly cause us setback or harm. The magnitude of forgiveness from our LORD for what we have done can <u>never</u> measure up to anything others could do to us. When we put forgiveness into practice, we are free from the bondage of bitterness and pain that imprisons us, a prison that disconnects us from life and its wonders which God has made for us.

Forgiveness is the only human force that can stop the disintegration of relationships. This is why it is so essential. This is why God forgives us. This is why our LORD calls us to forgive.

When we have been hurt, or you have hurt others—and we all have—open your eyes and realize that it is the call of the Christian to dispel these conflicts. It is our call and mandate to forgive! It is also in our best interest and one of our main avenues to marriage relationship contentment. Without forgiveness, our family, our growth and maturity with Christ, and our effectual life with others cannot be built!

We forgive because God has forgiven us. So, let it go, let it go. Allow me to say, let it go!

Key marriage tip: If you want to get the last word in an argument, apologize!

God calls us to operate within the parameters of forgiveness, love, and mercy.

When we do forgive, we have hearts filled with suffering and torment. This sets the tone of your home and for your children, reaching into future generations. This is why the Bible says "*the sins of the father pass to mutable generations*", because we repeat the bad behaviors by living with the consequences and teaching them in turn. The same passage also says, *the love of God passes on to a thousand generations* (Exodus 34:6-7).

How can we receive Christ's forgiveness and claim Christ as our Savior when we are unable to forgive one another? Only when we have a forgiving attitude, we will have a heart at rest and in peace!

What Forgiveness Looks Like

Do not let any unwholesome talk come out of your mouths, but only what is helpful for building others up according to their needs, that it may benefit those who listen. And do not grieve the Holy Spirit of God, with whom you were sealed for the day of redemption. Get rid of all bitterness, rage and anger, brawling and slander, along with every form of malice. Be kind and compassionate to one another, forgiving each other, just as in Christ God forgave you. Ephesians 4:29-32

You know that this Ephesians passage directly applies to your marriage! Taking our lead from Matthew, Chapter 18 (and various other Scriptures), we can see what God requires of us, and we can know the appropriate response regarding the different categories of forgiveness. We, as Christians, must extend ourselves to other people with love and that which flows out of love—forgiveness!

A new command I give you: Love one another. As I have loved you, so you must love one another. By this all men will know that you are my disciples, if you love one another. John 13:34-35

We are to love and forgive one another—period! No strings attached! This is the model we are to use to show God's love to the world! When we do not, our un-forgiveness becomes malice and actually grieves the Holy Spirit!

We should be clear on this. A healthy Christian marriage and life are built when we put aside the malicious traits of an evil, sinful nature, and embrace our spouse in respect and love with mercy. What comes out of love is the release of our feelings of betrayal and hurt. We are called to model kindness, love, empathy, and compassion to our spouse; out of these, forgiveness will flow. God wants us to get with it, to wake up, and seize the wonders and opportunities He gives us.

Why is God's Spirit grieved? An unforgiving attitude and its ugly rotten fruits choke us off from His wonders!

Key marriage tip: Let it go! You must practice forgiveness in grateful response to the awesome Truth that is Christ and so that you may be able to enjoy God's goodness. Top of the list: your spouse.

Ask yourself this question: How do I handle forgiveness?

How do you respond when others forgive you? What do you do with opportunities that our Lord has for you? We must realize the generosity of grace, and being in Christ, that we have is what we do not deserve. Our Lord does not want us to forgive begrudgingly; He did not forgive us with conditions and strings attached.

We as Christians must extend ourselves to other people with love. Forgiveness flows from love!

This should be clear to us. A healthy Christian family is one who puts aside the malicious traits of our evil sin nature. We model kindness, love, caring, compassion, and forgiveness. God wants us to get with it, to wake up and seize the opportunities He gives us (John 13:34-35).

Can I do this when my spouse is an idiot or non-responsive? YES!

First: Forgiveness is Hard (Isaiah 55:8-9). Forgiveness is hard because it demands a surrender of our rights, our feelings, the drive to get even. Forgiveness may even demand suffering of the person who was wronged. God is governed by righteousness, while desires and emotions drive us. God has a moral and virtuous purpose while our purpose is self-seeking. Look, you may be one of the finest people with virtue and goodness, but you are human. We are human, and we need God. We need His amazing grace shown in and through Our Savior. Every one of us. Especially when life is hard.

Second: Forgiveness is Complete (Colossians 3:12-14) Forgiveness is actually canceling a debt. Forgiveness is a declaration of a positive bankruptcy that once filed the creditor may not retrieve the debt, and it is wiped out. We need to see the cancellation of the debt as a write-off and not any form of embezzlement. When we forgive, we forget, we are to no longer even have the desire for restitution or pay back or punishment.

Third: Forgiveness is Costly (Luke 6:27-31) When we forgive, it may incur a cost to us, and we should realize and welcome it. Christ did not owe our debt, yet He paid it with a price we cannot fathom! We need not base forgiveness on our feelings and desires, but to focus what forgiveness is, as Christ gave us, as He was our example.

John 3:16 is the example of what forgiveness costs our Lord. Understanding this is hard even for the mature Christian: it is virtually impossible for the non-Christian since it goes against the common sense of society. It seems the suffering should be on the one who did the wrong. However, we must strive to understand John 3:16 and seek the enormity of it AND know that this will create the content home and be a beacon of witness to the Supremacy of Christ.

This is why the cost brought to our Lord is the greatest cost of all. We need to realize this and respond accordingly to one another (Psalm 32).

Key marriage tip: Character speaks for itself in the home first. Outside of the home, we never owe people an explanation or excuse to be the person that God called us to be. We just are to be godly for His glory!

Let's look at some of God's character verses so we know:

• God is governed by righteousness; whereas, desires and emotions drive us.

• God has a moral and virtuous purpose; our purpose is self-seeking.

• God's primary purpose in our lives is to bring us out of our self-destructive and self-seeking nature, and into the reclamation of redemption in Him; this is the work of Christ.

• God's thoughts are beyond our comprehension and imagination; therefore, we should rely on Him, and not on ourselves.

God's forgiveness is not some cheap markdown or bargain. The cost was immeasurable and beyond price. Paul, in Colossians 3:13, tells us to forgive freely, as Christ has forgiven us. We must be willing to forgive as Christ has forgiven us. We must be willing to bear the cost, just as our LORD did. Forgiveness demands a substitution. How could we ever back away from forgiving each other? If we do, it is a bigger insult to our LORD than for the non-Christian to turn his or her back on His Grace—*because we know better*. Remember, knowledge brings responsibility. We are blessed to have knowledge of the Truth of Our Lord and Savior, and we are responsible for living out that very Truth.

We need to offer forgiveness.

Do not be overcome by evil, but overcome evil with good. Romans 12:2

We must be willing to go to our spouse who offended us, and, both verbally and non-verbally, forgive them. If necessary, we are to then seek an appropriate reconciliation if it was something devious or grievous, using a third party like a pastor or counselor to mediate. We are to offer the real cherishing love and acceptance to them. Remember, you are not offering love to *what they did*. God desires that we be involved in growing positive and healthy marital relationships because the primary purpose of our existence is relationships— relationships with God first and then with others.

In a healthy marriage relationship, we can model, grow in, make known and glorify our Lord. This should be a driving force of who we are as Christians, saved by faith in Christ Jesus through the amazing Grace of God the Father.

Questions to challenge, inspire and equip you to be better in your commitment, love and marriage:

Read Psalm 32; Matthew 18:21-35; Luke 23:34; **Ephesians 4:32;** Colossians 3:13

1. What happens to our relationships with our loved ones and with God when we bow to being intolerant or refuse to forgive?
2. When have you been filled with a forgiving attitude the most?
3. In what situation did you fail to forgive your spouse when you should have? What would have happened if you did?

4. How would your marriage improve with more forgiveness?

5. What is an act or situation that you need to forgive? Now, think through the steps you need to take to put a forgiving attitude into action. Think of any more specific instances?

We must realize the generosity of Grace and being in Christ, which we do not deserve.

Keep in mind, God is a God of relationships: He in Three, and He in and with us all, His Children. God is centered upon relationships and committed to relationships. So, yes, you can make it work!

CHAPTER 17

Forgiveness Pursues

When they hurled their insults at him, he did not retaliate; when he suffered, he made no threats. Instead, he entrusted himself to him who judges justly. He himself bore our sins in his body on the tree, so that we might die to sins and live for righteousness; by his wounds you have been healed. 1 Peter 2:23-24

The refusal to forgive sets marriages in the tone of antagonism.

Because we become consumed with our hurts, we then suffer with the guilt and bitterness. Our personal and family life will dissolve, and our impact on friends, family, church and the community, as Christians, becomes a hindrance instead of a blessing.

I was watching one of those reality TV shows recently where a bunch of young people who were put into a nice beach house to live and work together. The show is about the drama and strife each one causes the other, and how they *do not* work it out. After all, if they were a big, happy family, it would not make good TV (or so I am told by a friend in that business). One young woman, in her early twenties, kept making the statement, "I refuse to forgive anyone for anything." In the episode I watched, the attention was centered on how she was alienating everyone in the house, shocking even the most liberal open-minded person. The result was that she ended up alone, hated by the others, and in rehab for addiction.

She would make a big deal if someone took her cookie, or gave her an objectionable look. She came across as a very sad and pathetic person, whose self-imposed code of conduct, created out of her pride and past hurts, made it impossible for her to make friends, build connections or cooperate with anyone in her life. She could not see that she was the problem; she refused to take any responsibility. In her interviews, she blamed everyone else for her problems. The sad fact is that this is typical behavior amongst many people today, even Christians in the church!

Key marriage tip: Control your pride! If you do this, then you will be on the winning side of faith, life, and harmony!

My friend, who was a producer for that show, allowed me to talk to her. My encounter with her was sad. I tried to communicate a positive encouragement to her and let her know I care and will listen. She was having none of that. With all her fame, money and opportunities, she was a very miserable person. A year after that episode aired, she was in a relationship with what she described as her 'dream' man.' Yet, because of her refusal to forgive, or move beyond her hurts, she was miserable, and they were breaking up.

Key marriage tip: Do not be critical or use foul or disparaging language; people need to be lifted up, not torn down, for healthy relationships. If you do feel tempted to tear down, stop for 24 hours and see what happens.

Forgiveness does not minimize the offense.

To help wrap our mind of what forgiveness is all about. We need to realize that when we forgive, we are not saying, "*Hey, that was OK*". The offense does not need to be accepted; however, we are to embrace the person who committed the offense. It is like sin; we are to hate sin, but we are still called to love the sinner—unless it continues, and they refuse to repent.

Forgiveness is not the approval of the wrong; it only offers the Grace of love, rather than vengeance.

Forgiveness may not bring us to the level of trust that we had before. If a spouse cheats on you, you are called to forgive and reconcile. There is no question that trust will be eroded, and will take time to rebuild. Just forgiving the offender will not bring instant restitution of the relationship; perhaps, the relationship will be severed completely. Imagine a business partner embezzles and causes you to lose the business. You are to forgive that person, as we previously discussed, but this does not mean you would enter into a business relationship with that person again.

God does not ask us to minimize the wrong, but He does call us to forgive the person. We are not to repay evil for evil, rather, we are to repay evil with good, just as our LORD did for us.

In marriage and in life, we will all make mistakes—intentionally or unintentionally. We all have hurt our spouses, and we have all been hurt; we are all in the same boat of doing life together. When we refuse to forgive them, it is like escaping the disaster of the sinking of the Titanic in a tiny lifeboat, only to poke holes in the very lifeboat that saved us. Yet, that is what so many of us do with our marriage; we sabotage the very vessel that will help bring us healthy relationships. Why do we do that? We hurt—someone has hurt us, we hurt someone else. Sometimes, we are so filled with pain that we intentionally or unintentionally seek to inflict that hurt upon friends and family.

What can we do?

We need to understand that, in Christ, we escape from the sinking ship because of our redemption, which we do not deserve. Christ gives us the vessel to be free and that vessel is *forgiveness.* Since everyone else in our family is in the lifeboat needs the cross too, why try to sink one another? All you will accomplish is the sinking of your loved ones and yourself.

Key marriage tip: When you forgive your loved one, you cut the cancer out of your relationship. If you do not forgive, your whole family will become malignant.

To stop the continual cycle of hurt, we have to step out of the sinking boat and be willing to forgive! We may get wet, but at least we will not drown!

As Christians who are saved by Faith in Christ through the Grace of God, we are still in the process of growth and sanctification. We are yet imperfect, no matter what our level of maturity. If you are thinking, *I refuse to forgive,* just as that young woman did, consider this reason to forgive. So few of us will actually forgive. From this unforgiveness for ourselves or for others, comes our pain, hurt, and resentment. This resentment escalates into animosity, and builds into bitterness, until it destroys relationships and causes us isolation, just as it did with that young woman on TV. She refused to forgive, and built an impenetrable wall that caused bitterness and isolation as she wallowed in her troubles, blaming everyone else for them. She would not allow forgiveness to break down the wall that would permit the building of life and relationships.

We must have the realization and the capacity to understand how much we have been forgiven by Christ!

Those who have been forgiven much must forgive those who did not do much to us. We do this in thanksgiving and in compassion to Who and why Christ did for us. We must know that we are forgiven, in order to forgive each other; this is crucial to the Christian experience. As our LORD continues to give us Grace and forgiveness, are not we to do the same with each other, our loved ones? We show ourselves to our family, church and world to be extremely foolish, selfish and prideful when we do not practice continual forgiveness!

We have to give up our perceived right of revenge and retaliation.

This can be a tough process, but one that we can accomplish through prayer and self-surrender. Try to look at it this way: The offense against you is actually an offense against God. As God's child, you are in His protection and care. When someone offends you, it also becomes an offense against God

Himself. In the cases of our spouses, please remember that they are God's children, too! Thus, we are to surrender our rights to His Lordship, and cancel the debt—completely out of existence and out of our hearts and minds.

Key marriage tip: To properly forgive your loved one, give it over as if it never happened. You will be surprised that once you do this, you will feel the load lifted off you and you can rest in the comfort of the Lord.

When you pray to God, you need to be actually requesting that He would take the desire of revenge away; then, relinquish your desires of revenge!

It is the responsibility of the person who did the wrong to repent—not the person offended. Thus, you cannot force your spouse to repent; you can only pray for him or her, and offer the forgiveness. Keep in mind that the relationship can only positively continue when repentance and forgiveness are pursued by both.

Key marriage tip: Forgiveness does not change what was done in the past. Forgiveness can heal and help further your relationship with your spouse!

If one of you refuses to repent, or refuses to accept the other's sincere forgiveness, this means their nature is in denial. They feel no wrong was committed, or see you as trying to manipulate their will or putting your pride is in the way, or they are just too hurt at the moment. Barring any mental disorder, they may enjoy inflicting hurt and hardship. In any case, the reason is not your responsibility, nor are you responsible for their acceptance. Your responsibility is only to genuinely offer them your forgiveness. We need to accept the fact of sinful human nature; some people just will not *play ball* God's way, especially some Christians. If this is the case with your forgiveness, then it still remains between you and Christ, as it is anyway, because we are God's children.

The end of all things is near. Therefore be clear-minded and self-controlled so that you can pray. Above all, love each other deeply, because love covers over a multitude of sins. 1 Peter 4:7-8

If you are the wrongdoer

If you are the person who hurt your spouse, you are not alone. We have, each and all, hurt someone. If your spouse is unwilling to forgive you, it is still up to you to make it right. You may not receive that forgiveness, but that is between them and God, and not you. What you need to do is go through the steps of forgiveness, but with the emphasis on earnestly repenting and offering restitution. You need to confess, openly (and maybe publicly with permission). Do not rationalize what you did, or minimize it in any way. Then, go to Christ, humbly and with a repentant attitude—which means, you make a commitment to change your heart, mind, and actions!

If going to your spouse is impossible because of distance, death, or restraining order, then we need to totally rely on God. Take your lead from 2 Corinthians 7:8-11. This allows Christ to be your Mediator. You are not completely off the hook from truly seeking repentance just because there is no face-to-face forgiveness. Just because you may not be able to physically go to them does not mean you do not have to forgive them or seek forgiveness. You can use a third party—maybe a pastor or a letter—and definitely seek forgiveness through repentance and prayer.

What about the big things like abuse, abandonment, and affairs? You may need a qualified counselor to guide you through. The party who sinned must repent and stop it. If not, get out. (As always, in case of danger, please call the police if needed.) The Bible may release you from the marriage; but to heal and move on, you may also build a better marriage. I have seen marriages become better than ever after a betrayal, because that drove both husband and wife closer to Christ. Hopefully you can get there without the sin and its consequences.

When we refuse to forgive or refuse to repent, then we are holding ourselves back from God and His best for us. We will lavish destruction and chaos on our family that may be repeated for many generations. We may rationalize the reality of the infection of sin, and its destructive nature to our being, and to those around us. We create a wall to shut ourselves off from God and one another. We turn on ourselves with the consequence, without any reprieve or comfort.

Hatred stirs up dissension, but love covers over all wrongs. Proverbs 10:12

What can I do? Take a serious look into Psalm 32. Meditate over it carefully, and then, surrender yourselves over to the love of Christ. Allow the sin to be forgiven and released. Be courageous. Seek out forgiveness and public confession and reconciliation. Allow yourself to grow and mature to be the best, whole person Christ desires for you to be. There is simply no better way. This is liberation and true comfort.

Key marriage tip: Give your spouse space. If they or you are in a 'mood,' back off and do not engage. Pray and wait for the right timing to have deep conversations. Remember, love is patient!

How many times must I forgive them? The Bible tells us it is continual. For Christ, there is no point beyond which our accumulation of sins becomes unforgivable. So, our response is to forgive others, especially our family, as there is no cap, or limit, or expiration to forgive. As followers of Christ, neither the intensity nor the number of wrongs should have an impact on us. If we were to place a limit, then our effect of building relationships would have a chain attached to it instead of having a chain reaction to grow. With a limit, you cannot grow (Luke 17:3b-4).

Key marriage tip: Be willing to cancel the betrayal!

How do I know I have forgiven my spouse properly? When you feel compassion toward them, even when wronged you, then you can be assured you did truly forgive them.

Let the precepts of our Lord impact and change you to the core of your being. Let the power of prayer be your focus, and the Scripture your heartbeat. Our standard is not that of the world, but that of God. We would not want to go through life and marriage in misery and bitterness, only remembering the hurts and wrongs, so we are harboring grudges, and experiencing unhappiness. This is not the plan that Christ has for us! Bitter people have no impact for the kingdom of God except to cause dysfunction in the home with division and distraction. They have the tenacity and drive to show everyone the hurts and wrongs they suffered. Do not let this happen to you, or to the people around you. Take your lead from this verse, not your inclinations (Romans 8:28-39).

Questions to challenge, inspire and equip you to be better in your commitment, love and marriage:

Read Psalm 32; Matthew 18:21-35; Luke 23:34; **Ephesians 4:32;** Colossians 3:13

Because what Christ has done for you, God's special and unfailing favor is being poured out for you. This favor is His love, kindness, and mercy. How have you accepted these, and put them into your life as well as the lives of your spouse?

1. How do you deal with anxiety and disappointments? What about when they come from your spouse?
2. What can you do to look to Christ for your perseverance? How will that set a better tone in your home?
3. Why must we keep ourselves tuned into God constantly and continually, and allow Him to carry us through? How does this help you to forgive?
4. Most Christians couples have a hard time fathoming God' capacity to forgive, and thus do not do so well when they need to forgive one's spouse. Why is that?
5. What can be done to show your loved ones Christ's love and forgiveness? Even if they do not show you?

How do I handle forgiveness? How do you respond when others forgive you? What do you do with opportunities that our LORD has for you?

CHAPTER 18

Marriage Money Matters

"The earth is the LORD's, and everything in it, the world, and all who live in it." Psalm 24:1

Money and marriage go together like ice-cream and a cone or a car and gasoline or more like this—problems and fighting.

Because financial issues can be so destructive in relationships, you need to know how to make sure both of you know what money is and how money works. How do we do this? Know that money is a tool, not the focus. It is important to have a good, biblical concept of how to deal with budgeting and debt. Know what comes in, know what goes out, and make sure the 'in' is more than the 'out'. Communicate without judgments and strings or pride to one another.

When you apply this knowledge, you have a plan, and you can do your best with it. Most conflicts in a marriage deal with finances because one or both parties have of a lack of communication and understanding of it. One likes to spend, one likes to save. One wants this and the other wants that. One does not want the other to have this or that. If one or both of you have a lot of debt (could be credit cards, student loans, or other things), you will have a fight and it escalates. You need to have a plan to deal with spending and debt. If there is debt, you must have a plan to pay the debt off (before marriage if possible). Regardless, it is necessary to have open communication about money matters, have a clear plan, and work toward the goal of working together. Do not be too prideful to get help!

Key marriage tip: Sixty percent of couples in marriage counseling, identify money as the major problem. Please, learn to control your money so it does not control you!

Make sure your goals are to solve any spending problems and money management issues. If just one of you cannot do this, you will have an immense amount of unnecessary problems in your marriage. A well-planned budget will help you greatly. There are plenty of good resources on how to do prepare and follow a good budget plant; these are just a few—any book by Larry Burkett or Ron Blue or go to Crown.org.

Key marriage tip: Make sure both of you know how money works. Have a good biblical concept on how to deal with budgeting and debt. Most conflicts in a marriage deal with finances! If you have an agreed-upon budget and you both are trustworthy in sticking to it, you have virtually eliminated a major source of conflict in many relationships.

All this is about one key biblical word, *stewardship*, which simply means to manage someone else's property. This is good news. As Christians, we know and should remember what Scripture proclaims—everything belongs to Go. We are to be good stewards, good managers of the property (blessings) of God that He grants to us. Since everything belongs to Christ, we need to have the attitude and view that our things are His things. Our stuff is really His stuff. Anything we have—including our bodies, time, talents, possessions, relationships—is the His.

Anything that we have ever had and will have is His. Look at it like this: We are mere lessees of the property, money, relationships, talents, time, and even our lives that God has for us. That means, all that we are and all that we have is not really ours to begin with. Everything belongs to God. Money is one of those things—a tool for us to exchange commodities, His possessions. Money is not ever supposed to be the end goal in our lives; money is a tool that can empower us and help us live in a certain way. Understanding and adhering to this biblical precept can be the biggest stress reducer and a calm maker in a marriage (Proverbs 3:9-10; Matthew 6:19-24; 1 Corinthians 4:2; Ephesians 5:15-16).

With stewardship and marriage, our duty is to learn how to become responsible stewards of the Lord's resources that are entrusted into our care. As a couple, we can do this together. We are to do is manage everything to the best of our abilities for Christ's glory.

Key marriage tip: Do not give to get; rather give to just give as Christ gave to you. Commit to the promise, "I will be more and do more," and see what happens.

In Matthew 6:19-24, we are told how to look to money and things. Living by this principle will make for a happy heart and a content home. Jesus plainly tells us, *"Do not store up for yourselves treasures on earth...For where your treasure is, there your heart will be also..."* This Bible passage warns us how possessions can divide our mind so that they control our direction in life. In so doing, they capture our hearts controlling our will and aspirations and affecting our homes and all of our relationships. It is true that we all need various kinds of possessions in order to live—food, housing, transportation, clothing, etc.—but we must remember who actually has ownership of these things and remember that we have the duty and responsibility to be good stewards.

Jesus is not condemning personal possessions; rather, He is challenging the focus of our hearts.

What if we just did not use money, got rid of it, and or lived without stuff? If we gave up everything, we would not be able to function in society, make a home livable, raise children, or be a blessing to others. Christ wants us to wisely use what He has for us, even have fun. At the same time, we cannot have our hearts set on possessions; we need to trust in our God as Provider; while being wise stewards. God provides us with all we need; it is our responsibility to work, using our gifts and abilities, and not be lazy. When we live for possessions, and we set our minds on the accumulation of wealth and things, we miss opportunities and marks He has for us, mainly the building of our family in Christ. Our hearts become divided. Our attention and devotion goes to things that have no real meaning, things that will rot away, while things of real, eternal value are ignored. The fleeting, controlling issues in our lives capture our will and time, while the real effectual intimacy and relationship building and calling of our family and the Church go unanswered and unaccomplished.

Do not store up treasures on earth: Possessions take a powerful toll on the human mind and home. They cause our focus to be distracted from our primary purpose and call, to create a fruitful home and to glorify our Lord. They mess up marriages, and ruin families, leaving us distorted in what is really important. Possessions can even cause corruption as they often lead people to do what is unscrupulous and depraved.

Later on, in Matthew, Jesus describes the difficulty of lovers of money entering the kingdom of Heaven. It is difficult, but not impossible. They have to overcome the desires that can easily enslave us! Be careful: Your marriage is more important that money and stuff! If it is not, you will go astray and feel empty. While wealth and riches are not evil in and of themselves, they can easily become "gods"—our main focus. The love of money, temptations of gathering wealth, and the desire to be rich has led astray and destroyed countless families over the centuries. Do not let it happen to yours (Matthew 19: 16-26; 1 Timothy 6:9-10; Hebrews 13:5)!

If your treasure is on earth, your heart will undergo many disappointments, and the storms of life will overwhelm you and hurt your family. All of the things in life in which you find your primary joy are suddenly gone!

Can you go through all of your possessions and tell which ones will rot and will not apply to your Christian growth? How can that list, motivate you to seek what is in Matthew 6:33? Then what will you have, do and feel (Matthew 6:33; 7:24-27; Luke 12:33-34; Hebrews 10:32-39; 1 Timothy 6:17-19)?

When our focus is on possessions, they become our idols, and we worship them. Our identity, and personification of who we are, becomes branded by what we have, and not who we are in Christ (1 John 5:21).

This is why Jesus tells us that, *you cannot serve two masters*. When your attention is divided, you cannot be attentive to either one and your spouse gets pushed away or even abused. In biblical times, servants and workers rarely had more than one manager. That would have been foolish, as their time, interests, and commitment would have been divided. When it did happen, it almost always meant disaster. This can happen when people try to work two jobs; although sometimes it is necessary for financial reasons, one's commitment will be divided. However, in our commitment to the Lord, He must be Lord, which means He is ruler over all.

Key marriage tip: We must not be afraid to find out what God's plan is and yield to it.

When we are seeking things outside of His parameters and precepts, especially with virtue and character, we will be dividing ourselves away from Christ and creating a dysfunctional home. When this happens, all of our Christian life will be affected. Those around us will get the wrong impression of Christ as He is reflected in a skewed way. Take a look at the key word, *Master;* by definition, *master* means and demands total loyalty. We cannot please two masters at the same time, especially with God. We have to choose whom we will serve and be determined to keep our promise and commitment (Exodus 34:14; Josh. 24:14-15; Ephesians 5:5; Colossians 3:5)!

Whom will you serve, and will you be determined to keep your promise and commitment?

Let's look at another key word, Fear the LORD means to trust, serve, and worship Him. Money and things can easily become the priorities in our lives! The choice becomes whether we will worship the One True God, or be *idolaters*, following after false gods. Know that our real and true treasures are imperishable! Make a list of them, and put them in a place that you can see daily to encourage yourself. Keep in mind that true treasures are not material in nature, so look to relationships and character (Proverbs 1:7; 3:5; Matthew 6:33; 1 Timothy 6:9-19; 1 Peter1:3-5)

Key marriage tip: Our marriages are to be mirrors to the Kingdom of God, to God's Glory and His purpose. Surrender to His Lordship, surrender your family and assets, your wants and needs to His love and care, and be the proper steward that loves, cares, has faith and is effectual!

Your personal life and family will succeed when you focus on Christ and not problems!

You must be able to ask questions, listen, and be vulnerable to reflect, challenge, and address each other's views and ideas on budgeting. Do not focus on faults, rather on areas that need growth. Take it slow and develop your budget first. If you do not do this, then you will be among the countless relationships in our culture filled with miscommunication, hurt, and misery!

Questions to challenge, inspire and equip you to be better in your commitment, love and marriage:

Read Proverbs 3:9-10; Matthew 6:19-24; 1 Corinthians 4:2; Ephesians 5:15-16

1. Why is it important that Jesus challenge us to the focus of our heart? What is that focus?
2. Have you had possessions that claimed your identity and devotion? How and why? What can you do to rid yourself of those false devotions?
3. Money is not for power and control, it is a tool for effectual living and our Lord's service! How can you make this your mindset? How will it improve your family?
4. How can possessions be used to point your life toward the positive, and help others?
5. What is the balance between your possessions being bad, yet being used for good?
6. Can you go through all of your possessions and tell which ones will rot, and will not apply to your Christian growth? How can that list motivate you?
7. How can your purpose in life be governed with godly goals and direction?

Make your budget, but first pray, and pray more and treat each other with respect, dignity, listen and take breaks, perhaps have fun doing it!

Remember, our real and true treasures are imperishable!

Praise be to the God and Father of our Lord Jesus Christ! In his great mercy he has given us new birth into a living hope through the resurrection of Jesus Christ from the dead, and into an inheritance that can never perish, spoil or fade. This inheritance is kept in heaven for you, who through faith are shielded by God's power until the coming of the salvation that is ready to be revealed in the last time. 1 Peter 1:3-5

See Appendix III for a plan.

CHAPTER 19

Divorce Proof Your Marriage

What causes fights and quarrels among you? Don't they come from your desires that battle within you? You desire but do not have, so you kill. You covet but you cannot get what you want, so you quarrel and fight. You do not have because you do not ask God. James 4:1-3

What is more important than compatibility? It is a cooperation!

There is no 100% certainty to guard yourself of everything; there are just too many variables in a sinful world. Do not despair, though; there are a few things we can do to best protect what is most vital and important that will echo into eternity, our family!

A better view of marriage will help your family greatly. A successful Christian marriage that works is a 'covenant' between two sinful, imperfect people redeemed by the Blood of Christ, who refuse to give up on each other. When we understand this, we can practice the two key marriage builders that are more effective than anything else. To love and to respect. This means we are to cherish our wives and respect our husbands, even when they do not deserve it. Because that is how Christ is with you for eternity (Genesis 2:24; Proverbs 3:1-35; Malachi 2:14-16; Hebrews 13:4)!

If we refuse to love and reject the respect, we will create a toxic environment that kills a relationship.

For successfully divorce-proofing your marriage, what we are doing is simple—practice cherishing love, respecting acceptance and praying together, so you really value your spouse. Two more things—guard your heart from lust and sin and control your pride! If you do these five things:

1. Love—cherish
2. Respect—value
3. Guard against lust
4. Control your pride
5. Pray together

…You and your spouse will be on the winning side of faith, family life and harmony!

Guard yourself against Lust!

It is easy to want something else, a better dress a better job or car, or a nicer home and so forth. Many you have been tempted into thinking you want a better spouse. If you have the means to work and set goals and honor God and be a wise steward, you can pursue more if that is an avenue where God is still first and foremost in your life. As to the spouse situation, please remember that a spouse is not a goal; your husband or your wife is created just like you—a beautifully and purposely created person made by God, living in a fallen world with all the foibles and faults, gifts and blessings that you also possess. In marriage, God has given you this person, and you vowed before Him to do love and honor them, forsaking all others in any time. Honor them! When lust comes knocking—and it will in our modern society, do not buy in! Do not rationalize that God says it is ok, that is just sin and your pride talking. Pray, and commit yourself to Christ. Pray. Read Scripture and pray, then pray some more and surrender it to the Lordship of Christ at the foot of the Cross (**Matthew 19:6**; Luke 16:18).

Key marriage tip: Talk about your day with one another and listen. Not every detail, like what pantyhose you buy or every detail at work, just commune and listen. If they do not understand what you are explaining, then share why this is important; restate it in a different way.

Communicate and Commune! Talk. Listen. Talk. Listen. Then talk and listen some more. This is not just a cliché; it is the essence of relationships.

Everything we have talked about in building your marriage are from the avenues of God's true Truths to help you grow in your spousal relationship and be effectual to your loved ones. It all comes down to this: We must see our lives as belonging to Christ as LORD. We must see each other how He wants us to see it, as an expression of character, honor, wonder, and gratitude to God for who He is and what He has done. Our marriage can express our praise and honor for His glory. As a Christian, you are in Christ, we are like a bride married to a groom, as Israel was a bride of God. Marriage is a celebration of our salvation in Him (Matthew 5:12; Revelation 21:2).

Allow Christ to be the lead of your heart and then your marriage!

Remember, the main reasons why marriages fail is because our communication breaks down! Why? Because we are not properly loving and respecting and thus not listening and or speaking with kindness. All because our pride is running amuck and or we are lusting after something else! Or we are stuck in hurt and unforgivness. Thus, to succeed in marriage and in life, we must be willing to rise above ourselves in order to listen with openness and the nonjudgmental understanding of our spouse.

Here are some Divorce Proof Tips and Marriage Builders:

A mature Christian has a heart that is formed, focused, and straightened in and from our growth in Christ. We must have a heart of conviction in Christ, flowing with gratitude for Who and What He has done, with vitality, power and authority to take our lead from Christ. This is all about what we have talked about with a heart that is focused upon Christ as the foundation of our marriage. In Him, you can get through anything! Our goal, instead of wanting someone new, might be to better to hear His precepts to edify and love the people in our family, especially our spouse. This enables us to commune. How do we do that? Read the Bible, pray, pray together, grow in your spiritual formation, pray with your family and get support doing this when it is broken.

Divorce-proof tip: Marriages that are in trouble tend not to pray together or communicate nor do they spend time together. When this happens, it is time to refocus and reboot and get help.

Divorce-proof tip: Have a disagreement or a problem to solve; then, listen to their position. Be kind!

Divorce-proof tip: Never say anything negative about your spouse in public! Misery does not like company, and you will get bad advice back. Remember to love and respect. Only talk to a trusted friend or qualified pastor or counselor, and let your spouse know about it, (unless there is abuse).

Divorce-proof tip: Never drop bombshells in public that you have not discussed previously with your spouse. Like, *I got a new job, and we are moving.* Not good! Discuss first, and then tell others.

How do you do these things if your spouse seems distant, overly hurt, will not try or has given up. Here is your ministry. Be there, act in love and be consistent, and pray and pray. Look over all the tips in this book and do them. This will take time, you are not in a 30-minute TV show with a nice and neat resolution. Think long term with baby step results.

Divorce-proof tip: Show interest. Put your newspaper, magazine, phone or smart electronic device down when you talk, out for dinner and so forth. Real life lived in the present always supersedes media and virtual life!

Remember, everyone needs their down time and time to be alone to reflect, refresh. Give them space, take your space. You do not need to be together all of the time. The opposite is true, too; do not spend too much time apart. The amounts?

It is different for each couple. Communicate and practice; see what works.

Divorce-proof tip: When you fight, and you will have disagreements and problems, you have to take a step back away from the emotions and ask yourself, is this important? Is my point important enough to hurt my family?

Divorce-proof tip: When you are fighting, remember you already lost. Focus on how to resolve it and listen.

Divorce-proof tip: Plan ahead your disagreements. That is, have a plan how to handle each others point of view when you disagree and do that when you are not disagreeing.

Divorce-proof tip: When we realize that marriage is not about me, *what I want, what my spouse can do for me*, then, we are moving up in our relationship and will get more out of it and be more content.

Do you have the same argument about the same things over and over again?

My dear brothers and sisters, take note of this: Everyone should be quick to listen, slow to speak and slow to become angry...James 1:19

Think about what makes sense to you and also how the other person might view the situation. Just because it seems sensible to you doesn't mean the other person will see it this way. So, pray, rethink and go about it like this. Go to a neutral area like a park and have a walk and talk about it and comment to solve it. Say, We *have this problem, let's make it an opportunity, how can we both solve it or come to a mutual respect over it? What are your thoughts or our steps, what we need to do?*

Divorce-proof tip: Major on the majors, don't major on the minors i.e. it is more important that you pray together than how the house is organized. It is more important to practice love than what color you should paint the bathroom...

Divorce-proof tip: Give compliments, give kind words of affirmation, make them feel special, even when you do not feel like it. We all need to feel loved, give the love you want in return and it may happen.

Divorce-proof tip: Do not just criticize or always talk about yourself, refocus on being positive with your spouse.

Remember, men and women think differently and act and react differently. This is good. You are different, that is OK, you would not want to be married to yourself! Celebrate and respect differences and work on your own character and be an example.

Have a budget!

See the previous chapter on this and Appendix III. How much is coming in and how much is going out? Make sure what comes in is more than what goes out and agree upon it. Have an agreement on how much money each person is allowed to spend on their own, beyond what is budgeted for. What are the limits for bigger purchases and let the other know before spending the amount you agreed upon is the limit.

When you buy gifts for one another, they do not need to be expensive. But, put some thought into it and try harder for something special and unique to them. Waffle makers and ties just do not cut it, they do not say you are special to me, neither does expensive jewelry. Remember, you can't buy love, it is leased through our Lord.

Do not forget about intimacy and romance.

Women, especially need to be romanced and wooed, even after fifty years of marriage. Men, we may not admit it, but men like this, too. So, practice and respond to one another. If you have kids, get away for a date night once a week. Do not use sex as a weapon or tool to manipulate. If one of you can't perform, see a medical doctor first, then a counselor.

Divorce-proof tip: Make your marriage a priority and work it as it is. Spend time, quality time, date nights, treat them with kindness and the Fruit of the Spirit.

Divorce-proof tip: Be romantic! Do not be boring! Remember the excitement when you first were dating and try to be that exciting person who is interested in your spouse. Try to create memorable moments, plan fun stuff, get away, do not always do the same old things.

Divorce-proof tip: If things get stale, then be stimulating, try a hobby together, volunteer somewhere together, find some fun together.

Marriage should never get old and stale, if it seems to, try new and different routines and things. Marriage is work; keep working at it and remember we are created to work and work was instituted before the fall of humanity and before sin entered into the world. So, that means "work at it" and have fun doing so.

Guard against lust! I might have said that before, and I will say it again.

In times of hurt and conflict, we must remain faithful as betrayal is then most powerful killer to any relationship. Sin is made to look fun and enticing in movies, even romantic, but in real life that very same celebrity who portrayed a romantic cheat, is devastated when they are cheated upon, and that ends their relationship. So, do not do it (Proverbs 6:26-33; 7:24-28; 18:13; Matthew 5:27-28; 1 Corinthians 6:9; 16-18).

Divorce-proof tip: Do not flirt, period. It is not harmless! That is the prime gateway to affairs.

Sexual encounters are the obvious way to be unfaithful. But, there are other ways in which we cheat on our spouse. This usually employs our time and talents away from family and where they are supposed to be. Like, flirting, sexting, sharing private pictures or videos, it is wrong if you are married, period! That also means on online, social media, anywhere in cyberspace, the workplace, at school, or in real life, do not flirt.

Divorce-proof tip: Do not confide with the opposite sex with any personal encounters or moments or anything your spouse would not approve of.

Also, do not share what your intimate secrets you have with your spouse to others. This also means to do share other deep secrets, like marriage problems or childhood traumas or dreams to the opposite sex unless you are sharing them with a trusted counselor. What do we learn?

Divorce-proof tip: Do not linger with people of the opposite sExodus Do your job with kindness, worship in a respectful mode; but, do not hang out, unless your spouse is there.

Divorce-proof tip: Develop healthy friendships with the same sex. Your spouse is not designed to fulfill your entire social life. Make friends, too. The secret to making friends is simple, be friendly and interested in them.

Divorce-proof tip: Watching pornography is not harmless or humorous like the movies and TV depict. It is extremely destructive to your mind's eye, and what you see is not even real. It will replace effectual reality with what is fleeting, and will sneak and snake its way into your relationship and cause havoc.

206 Dr. Richard Joseph Krejcir

Divorce-proof tip: Do not do what your spouse would not approve of. Do not do what you do not want your spouse to do. This will help you make wiser choices.

Divorce-proof tip: Get help when you need it even if you do not want it. See a qualified counseling pastor or therapist. There is not shame is seeking help, it is what God wants you to do!

Consider that real love is sacrificial. Our call as Christians is to go further than what our expectations, pride, hurt or the world expects.

First, like anything worth doing, you have to be willing to do it. Learning anything takes desire, time, effort, and practice. You have to want a healthier marriage, you need to work on better communication. You have to know what it means to cherish and what love is not, what is respect and what is contempt. You have to see what God has for you, not just what you want. Then, you have to want it to get it.

To answer before listening—that is folly and shame. Proverbs 18:13

Divorce-proof tip: Remember, forgiveness as Christ has forgiven you!

Divorce-proof tip: Never use or say the word 'divorce,' or *it would be better if we never been married.*

God's true Truths will help you grow in your spousal relationship and be effectual to your loved ones. It all comes down to this: we must see our life as belonging to Christ as LORD. He wants us to see it as an expression of character, honor, wonder, and gratitude to God for who He is and what He has done. Your marriage can express our praise and honor for His glory.

Questions to challenge, inspire, and equip you to be better in your commitment, love and marriage:

Read Proverbs 3. More passages to consider: Malachi 2:14-16; Matthew 19:6; Luke 16:18; Ephesians 5:15-16; Hebrews 13:4

1. Look carefully at Proverbs Chapter 3 and what God is saying. How can these Proverbs help you in your marriage?
2. Look at key phrases like:

   - *My son, do not forget my teaching, but keep my commands in your heart, for they will prolong your life many years and bring you peace and prosperity.*
   - *Let love and faithfulness never leave you;*
   - *Trust in the LORD with all your heart and lean not on your own understanding;*
   - *Do not be wise in your own eyes...*
   - What can these Proverbs do to help you never bring up the 'D' word (divorce)?

3. Why is using that 'D' word as a threat so destructive?
4. How can you better Communicate and Commune with your spouse?

5. How can you better guard yourself against lust? Remember accountability!
6. How can you better cherish and respect your spouse?
7. How can you better value your spouse?
8. How can you better control your pride?

CHAPTER 20

The Marriage Tune-up!

Let the peace of Christ rule in your hearts, since as members of one body you were called to peace. And be thankful. Let the word of Christ dwell in you richly as you teach and admonish one another with all wisdom, and as you sing psalms, hymns and spiritual songs with gratitude in your hearts to God. And whatever you do, whether in word or deed, do it all in the name of the Lord Jesus, giving thanks to God the Father through him. Colossians 3:15-17

Look to God's precepts for building a great marriage.

The practice of Christianity is a journey of our faith development as we encounter more of Christ through our learning and discoveries from His Word. We can also discover from our discipleship in Him. We grow in our knowledge and faith but we are not always ready for the deeper truths until we understand the basics and foundations. There are many truths and precepts in God's Word to be discovered and applied into our lives, marriages, and churches.

Marriage is not about pursuing one's happiness; rather, it is about how we continue the work of God in your marriage. Only then the happiness will come.

Key marriage tip: Selfishness will never make you happy, and you can't expect others to fulfill only what Christ can. Please do not expect your spouse to fulfill you;

rather, seek how to be less self-centered and more centered on how to build your family up. Only then will you be more fulfilled and happy.

The question we need to ask to stimulate a great marriage is this: Will you live out your Christian life into your marriage, even when things get tough? This will be a prime motivator to build a legacy of many generations of successful marriages, doing it, modeling it and keep it up in times of doubt, frustrations, hurts and setbacks.

Key marriage tip: God calls us to "cleave," not leave. Be the glue that sticks one another together.

In a triumphant marriage, what we are doing is simple, the practice of cherishing love and the acceptance of respect so you are both valuing each other. In this, you will be on the winning side of faith, family life and harmony!

1. Love—cherish
2. Respect—value
3. Guard against lust
4. Control your pride
5. Pray together

Remember, love confirms the authenticity of Jesus' and His followers!

Show me a marriage where there is real love, and I will show you a marriage that is connected with Christ and a family that is connected with one another, resulting in a marriage that is a power in the church and community! Show me pride and lust, I will show you dysfunction and strife.

In your marriage, there is a The Responsibility To Do Good!

First Peter Chapter 3 gives us the primary theme to make a better purpose of marriage in functioning and in joy. As we stated in previous chapters, basically there are two main themes that tie together. The first is the essential role of the husband whose call, is to love, as in cherish his wife intimately, and with precious care. We are called to see her as precious and not take her for granted.

Key marriage tip: You must embrace good listening and communication. Just be willing to listen without speaking and care enough to love enough to make this happen. Good, lasting marriages are built on communication; divorce is the result of the breakdown of our hailing frequencies.

The second theme is like a bookend holding up the theme of obedience to God, and by His call and lead, harmoniously relating to others. This is the theme of submission. Remember, real submission breeds closeness when it is formed from love. If it is subjugated, such a barrier to God is formed that even our prayers will not be heard! Thus, compassion, care, and love pave the way to effective, relational harmony and blessing from God. Pride and our strong-willed attitude set up a barrier, making all we do ineffective, destructive, and meaningless. If we want God to be attentive to us, we must do our part by being attentive to others without iniquity (1 Peter 2:1-12).

Lasting and happy marriages are about finishing the Word that God has begun in you both! Philippians 1:6

This is not about being served or even serving each other; rather, it is about co-serving with God to each other and for others! This is to be a partnership, not a dictatorship. The theme poses the question *do we see our spouse as someone just to take care of our needs or do we see her as our helpmate and co-laborer with Christ?*

In a godly marriage, we are stewards of the precious love that God has extended to us; it needs to flow from us to other people in our lives, especially a spouse. This is to be our utmost responsibility, and done with care. It is a call to careful, steadfast love, like caring for a precious, priceless object (1 Peter 3: 1-12).

Key marriage tip: To create the effective triumphant marriage depends on our heart and will to put it into play. Just thinking about it or postponing it or waiting for the other to respond will not bring a good marriage.

To clarify, submission is respect, and thus is not to exceed the parameters of the will of God or of love and righteousness. As an example, submission is not an excuse to batter or put one's wife down in any way. In this passage, Peter was originally speaking to converted wives who had unbelieving husbands; now, it is the other way around. The directive to husbands is even more daunting than that given to the wives! Husbands are called to *love*, which is much greater in importance and prominence than submission!

Real love is what sets the tone and standard for the relationship.

This is all framed in the key phrase, *be considerate* refers to treating a spouse with the utmost care and love. Because, submission is also a response! Because the husband loves, because the husband cares, because the husband puts his wife's best interests forward, the wife submits, and he earns her devotion. It is the husband's responsibility to set the tone of love and care! Keep in mind that this was called for in a time and culture that considered women lower than farm animals! It was taught in a culture where the "alpha" male (i.e. the lead man of the family) ruled in absolute dominance for order, organization, structure, protection, and community.

Key marriage tip: There will be change! Anticipate change, prepare for change, realize life is always changing. This is good, what is wrong can be set right or just will be temporary. Life becomes an adventure as you grow. There are the stages of life, careers, moving, kids, aging, health, family, life and death, there will always be change, your spouse will change, so will you, beware, embrace it, be willing to adjust and you will triumph through it with your focus on Christ.

The mandate to love (1 Corinthians 13:4-7) was, and still is to some, an extreme wake-up call that commands the husband to thoroughly exhibit all of the qualities of biblical character in his relationship with his wife.

It is my sincere prayer that you are both in a solid, growing, Christ-centered relationship! If not, be willing to build one. Too many Christians have given up on godly values and caved in to desperation and desire when it comes to marriage. They just want someone and when they do not satisfy, they are given up like a worn out coat. Mend the coat, fix it, and make it better than new! I have seen this cycle, over and over for years and years, and people just do not seem to learn, or else just do not want to get it. They end up in dysfunctional relationships and pass those dysfunctions on to their children, and the cycle goes on! Marriages could be so much more wonderful, so romantic and solid, if only God's values and precepts were brought into it.

Key marriage tip: Before you react to something, take some time out to pray and think it through first.

Do not let yourself become a statistic, imprisoned in a world of stifle and chaos, when God has such a better plan for you.

Key marriage tip: Talk about how you will handle disagreements and conflict, when you are not having a quarrel.

Remember that the prime key to building a healthy marriage is this: Love is reciprocal!

The husband loves and the wife responds with respect and honor—in the midst of their relationship with Christ as LORD!

Christ and the church are the prime models for us in a lifelong commitment of monogamous marriage.

Key marriage tip: Seek Christ, place Him first and foremost in your life, and He will provide. Seek yourself, and you will be sad and lonely in so many ways! Remember that the heart of any healthy relationship is love and respect!

Hebrews 13 tells us that we can do it, we can love. We can treat others as Jesus does: feel their pain, have compassion, and do something to help. We can also give honor to our marriage, even helping others to build their marriages and fight against immorality and adultery.

Key marriage tip: We are not to love money, but regard it only as a tool; we are to be content in Christ, for He will never leave or forsake us.

We can have confidence in Christ, for He will help us; we need never be afraid of situations or peoples. We are not in this life or our marriage alone; we have Christ and one another. He gives us all we need to run this race of life and faith successfully. Do not forget to respect your leaders, receive the Word from them, and remember all of the good.

Jesus is the same yesterday, and today, and tomorrow— forever.

In the *marriage bed*

A key word in Scripture, the *marriage bed,* means the personal, intimate relationship of a man and wife which adultery, prostitution, and now pornography will defile. The word meant a virgin's bed where no one had sat on until her husband came into her life. The context is that the Church is a called to teach God's values, not compromise with the world, and to strengthen marriages and families by role modeling, encouragement, and help (1 Corinthians 7:3-5; Ephesians 5:22-33).

Remember, sexual immorality will seek to destroy what God has put together. This is a grievous sin and destroys. Thus, God calls us to guard against lust and whatever else destroys relationships and marriages. Sexual immorality is extremely dangerous. When Jesus walked and talked, when the New Testament was written, the Roman and Greek civilization was very loose morally, which led to their fall. So, what did Jesus focus on to circumvent this culture? He focused on knowing and modeling authentic love.

Key marriage tip: We are called to be careful of the love of money call to be, for while wealth and riches are not evil in and of themselves, they usually will become evil as they become our "god!"

The love of money, temptations of gathering wealth, and the desire to be rich has led astray and destroyed countless people over the centuries! We are called to be content with what He provides and not bend to greed or coveting. The point is that our real and true treasures are imperishable and eternal. Thus, our security is who we are in Christ, not what we have or want of money and/or "things." How one handles his finances are a real reflection of their spiritual life (Matthew 6:19-34;

19:16-26; Luke 12:15, 21; Philippians 4:10-13; 1 Timothy 3:3; 6:6-19; 1 Peter 1:3-5)!

How do we know we can do this?

God leaves us a us promise that He will never leave you. We have freedom from fear, as our Lord is our partner in life and faith. This was a great comfort that was originally given to a people in distress. Thus, a good marriage, a contented marriage, a triumphant marriage is centered on how we are trusting in our Lord! A bad marriage is centered on when we trust in other things, like hurts and fears or hopes and plans.

Key marriage tip: If you just focus on your hurts and losses, you will not be able to focus on Christ and making a better marriage.

We are called to love and to continue to do so no matter what the circumstances or oppositions.

Key marriage tip: "I am sorry," are the pleasantest words you can ever say to simulate that connectives and restoration!

Our confidence is in Christ and not our situations (Deuteronomy 31:6-8; Jos. 1:5; 2 Chron. 15:2; Psalm 37:28).

Questions to Ponder Together

Read Psalm 86 ; **Matthew 19:6 and** Hebrews 13:4. More passages to consider: **Genesis 2:24;** Malachi 2:14-16; Luke 16:18; Ephesians 5:20-33

This chapter is designed to be used as can be used for a church marriage retreat, a seminar, or a personal retreat with your spouse. If using it for a class, it is best to have your class read this book first. Then, have your class or retreat. You can go away for the weekend or do a little day by day. The important thing is to commit and realize that love is a choice and not a sensation.

1. How do you react to certain situations with your spouse? How should you? How would your spouse like you to react? How would Christ want you to react?
2. Read Psalm 86 slowly and carefully. Then, read it again in prayer, and then read it as a prayer.

   a. Now try this with your spouse and ask each other *how is this like us?*
   b. Go verse by verse asking *how is this like us* and *how can it be like us?*
   c. *Where are we in this?*
   d.. *Where do we fail?*
   e. *Where do we thrive?*
   f. *Where would we like to be?*
   g. *What do we need to do?*
   h. *How can the principles of this Psalm help heal our marriage?*
   i. *What are we going to do about it?*

3. Each spouse asks the other:

- What would you like to see happen in my heart?
- What do you think God would like to see happen in our hearts?
- What is 'your' goal for our marriage?
- Do you feel it is possible to get there? What do you think it will take? What do I need to do?
- How can we be better at our love and respect?

4. Pray!!! Keep spending time in prayer and commit to pray for your spouse when you first wake up, when you go to bed and throughout the day! Now also see if you can pray with your spouse, too—at least 5 minutes a day to start. If they are not open to it, do not push it, just pray for it.
5. Keep reading the 'marriage tips' in Appendix I. I have researched these for over twenty years, and wrote them, and I too have to read them often. We all need reminders and encouragement.

Keep in mind that a good soldier is willing to die for his or her country. Are you willing to live for your spouse and Lord? If so, we can come together and be committed to solve our problems. If not, we will fail our marriage and disappoint our Lord and Savior!

The Lord is my helper. A quote from the Psalms to encourage people not to be afraid, but to put their confidence and trust in the Lord (Deuteronomy 31:6-8; Psalm 56:11; 118:6; Philippians 4:11-12; Hebrews 2:15; 4:16; 11:23, 27).

Yes, you can have a wondrous marriage!

APPENDIX I

Marriage Tips

'Love the Lord your God with all your heart and with all your soul and with all your mind and with all your strength.' The second is this: 'Love your neighbor as yourself.' There is no commandment greater than these." **Mark 12:30-31**

Here is the list, over a hundred and twenty-five, of all the marriage tips that are given plus a few more. The first few in my opinion are the most important, the rest are in no particular order, all are useful and will change your marriage and life. They are designed to help focus you in the right direction, give practical help and encouragement. How to use them? Perhaps, read and practice one each day. Then when you are done, rinse and repeat.

We must have the desire to make marriage work regardless of how we feel or what we can see. We have to *want* to be in a good marriage to *have* a good marriage.

What we have been talking about may seem difficult, and perhaps even overwhelming, but take this to heart: *God does not call you to do anything that He has not empowered and enabled you to do!* The cross is the proof of how far He will go for you!

These marriage tips are from my musings and gathers form over thirty years of journeying through the Word of God. I do not know where they come from other than God is working in me and my mistakes, I suppose because they are true and based on His Word. Most come from my readings in Scripture, then I write down a thought from devotions or teaching perpetrations or from my blunders or from the advice of others. Some from a memory when I need an idea, some from the years of research I did.

Here is the complete list. These four points are the most important:

If you want your home content, then cultivate affection for one another and we do this by,

1. Real love means we will cherish our spouse!
2. Real respect means we will value our spouse!
3. Guard against lust, focus on your spouse not others!
4. Control your pride or it will control your home for sin!

…Then you will be on the winning side of faith, family life and harmony!

Communicate and Commune!

First, read 1 Corinthians 7:1-11, 39-40, 13:1-13, be committed to learn, forgive and engage God's Truth and apply His precepts to your life. Then, the revolution for the healthier marriage begins.

Tips for Husbands: If your wife does not respect you, you need to earn it and be patient. Some women will not voice their hearts, so you must discover what it is important and work on the following:

- Women need to feel loved, cherished, safe and protected.
- Listen to her and seek to deeply understand her, let her know you are glad that she is your wife.
- Discuss your feelings. Yes, it is hard, but it is necessary to share your hopes, fears, and dreams.
- Let her know that she is the most precious and the special person to you.
- Be romantic with non-sexual ways, special dates, and simple kind gifts like a flower with a note in her car.
- Find out what it is what makes your wife happy and do it, even if you do not, like hiking.
- Turn away from lustful images!
- Step up; take the role of leadership without condescending or lording over.

Tips for Wives: Even if your husband does not seem to cherish you or say what is important to him, you can help turn him on to you with the following:

- Express real lovingly respect and admiration, even if he does not deserve it; he may step up to it.
- Men tend to be prideful; do not keep pointing out past mistakes. Allow him to lead without saying, "I told you so." If he is wrong, respectfully suggest an alternative solution.
- Take notice of the good that he does and show your appreciation for the things he does right.
- Be more enthusiastic about sex and allure him, men like to be admired and pursued too.

- Find out what it is what makes your husband happy and do it, even if you do not share the same interests.
- Be patient; do not have unrealistic expectations!

Remember, if you want a great Christian marriage get this: There is nothing more important to a man than to feel respected and appreciated. There is nothing more important to a woman than to feel loved and cherished! Get this, and you get a good marriage!

Key marriage tip: The key is to be in prayer and find a way to develop your relationship to be respectful and loving.

Key marriage tip: Remember real love is sacrificial. Our call as Christians is to go further than what our expectations, pride, hurt or the world expects.

Key marriage tip: A successful Christian marriage that lasts is between two imperfect people in Christ, who refuse to give up on each other just as Christ never gives up on us.

Key marriage tip: The number one reason Christian marriages survive and succeed is a mutual respect for one another and a surrender to the Lordship of Christ.

Key marriage tip: See your marriage as a legacy, especially with children. So your godliness and character is played forward and multiplies by family, friends and all that observes you. Be to God's Glory in all you do!

Key marriage tip: See and practice your marriage as an offering to our Lord. To be poured out to Him so it affects all of our relationships. The learning and exercising of your faith will be the prime way of building your relationship and cherishing and respecting your spouse, even in difficult situations.

Key marriage tip: The number one reason why marriages fail is because of the breakdown in communication. To succeed in marriage and in life is to listen and be willing and open to the understanding of your spouse and others.

Key marriage tip: Your spouse is not an enemy, not an obstacle, not a setback, not a competitor, not a 'them;' rather a 'we.' When you are married you are in the 'our' business, not the 'them' or 'me' business. With a 'we' you become a success, with a 'me' and 'them' approach you will wither away.

Key marriage tip: When a successful marriage lasts between two imperfect people, it is because they refuse to give up on the work of the Lord.

Key marriage tip: We must allow Christ to be the leader of our heart and our marriage!

Key marriage tip: Before you react to something, take some time out to pray and think it through first.

Key marriage tip: Remember the health of our marriage will not only 'affect' (influence) you and your spouse, but also has 'effect' (result) on your children, family, extended family, church, friends, acquaintances and the reputation of our Lord. What you do and say does matter, and it is watched!

Key marriage tip: A wondrous marriage does not just happen. You have to work it. You must push forward, and move away from pride and into the Fruit of the Spirit. Cultivate communication and listening to each other. You will have set backs, so always play it forward, play it hard and push in love.

Key marriage tip: You cannot trust your heart; you can only trust the Lord!

Key marriage tip: If you do not have a mentor, now is the time to find one—preferably an older couple who have walked in faith for a significant period of time.

Key marriage tip: Remember, you can't change your spouse. You can only change yourself. The work begins in you first—without your seeking control of another. The work begins with you learning how to truly love and loving another.

Key marriage tip: The Christian life is meant as a journey to live with the goal of leaving behind a legacy of real love. This life of our's was never meant to be lived in the darkness of selfishness and pride.

Key marriage tip: Do not let your pride and hurt control you; rather, allow Christ' love to motivate you!

Key marriage tip: When love prevails in the midst of marriage, especially in times of strife and disagreement, it presents to God and each other a willingness to heal.

Key marriage tip: Pursuing love in the midst of one's toil is the irrefutable mark of a true follower of Jesus Christ!

Key marriage tip: Love is a journey and a process. You learn each of the characteristics of love, as knowing them, eternalizing them, accepting them, to practice them and allow the time in others to the learning curve. And remember, it is a continual adventure, not a destination.

Key marriage tip: Marriage is not a 50-50 split; rather it is a call to go the extra mile. If you only count your cost, then you are not counting on the Lord!

Key marriage tip: Yes, you can love and be loved, and we can make it work with the key of knowing Christ and applying His real, effectual love and grace.

Key marriage tip: Help each other realize they are irreplaceable. Encourage and inspire one another's hopes and dreams and to live the adventure of life well.

Key marriage tip: Show concern and care. Ask about their day. Who did they talk to, what did they learn? Speak without jealousy or condescending remarks or attitude. Listen! <u>Care enough to hear and uplift</u>. Listen first before offering any ideas or solutions. Put the care into your spouse as you would put into a nice car or a pair of shoes!

Key marriage tip: Marriages break up when you stop sharing, stop communicating, stop listening, and start assuming. Remember, communication is a 'requirement,' an 'always' and 'have to' it is not an 'elective,' you have to work on it.

Key marriage tip: You must get a grasp on grace and how Christ loves us; if you do not, you will only live with problems, and you will regress in distress.

Key marriage tip: Real love is cherished. This makes the marriage work, and you have to choose to do it and play it forward. This love in action must take us beyond ourselves and into the other person. When we fully understand what love is and dedicate ourselves to practice it, then we will have a thriving and content marriage!

Key marriage tip: Recognize each other's boundaries! You know the buttons; do not push them! Instead, honor and value them as God's child to respect them enough to love them enough.

Key marriage tip: Be grateful to the Lord, be patient, and remember real love is a choice—you have to work at it. Our maturity and growth in Christ will facilitate this, then you can be better committed to making it work, no matter what.

Key marriage tip: Yes, we need to detox from our day, but, do not come home just tied and plop in front of the TV, rather greet your family and spend time with them first. Need to wind down? Then, spend 10 minutes in your car or place of work or school and pray before entering your home.

Key marriage tip: Before you give up on your spouse, try harder, pray, and think it through.

Key marriage tip: Before you criticize or blame, take some time out to pray and think it through first.

Key marriage tip: Have something to say? Before you talk, make sure you are listening. No one, even your spouse, cares what you have to say if they are not cared for and heard first.

Key marriage tip: Do not always be blaming, criticizing, complaining and nagging, as these rotten fruits will never work. Show love by being kind.

Key marriage tip: You do not have to be in control, only The Sovereign Lord is in control…Unless you created the universe, let it go and allow your control to be yielded over to the Lordship of Christ. Your life and marriage will vastly improve.

Key marriage tip: You do not have a legitimate need to impress others. A real impression is not what you have; rather how you are—Fruit of the Spirit.

Key marriage tip: You do not have to be always right. Let it go, and focus on being right in Christ!

Key marriage tip: Laugh! Do not be afraid to laugh. In the best, happiest and long-lasting marriages, the couples laughed a lot. So, do not take yourself too seriously; be able to laugh!

Key marriage tip: Be a person who extols—that is to affirm and encourage others—especially your family member. Be a person who takes the cue to be unto Christ and follow His example—to love and care with excellence and fortitude.

Key marriage tip: If you are willing to live out the art of loving, then, you will keep your marriage alive and even thrive!

Key marriage tip: To create the best Christian marriage, this is essential: Men are to set a tone of love and be the head servant of the family; women are to respond to that love with respect and set the tone for a vibrant home.

Key marriage tip: Allow individuality, do not be so pushy on your personal, non-important preferences, like hair styles, dress, music, movies, and TV; just work on being appropriate and presentable and honoring each other's time. Negotiate the differences and remember respect.

Key marriage tip: Real respect and love are essential; we are called to right submission! Christ and the church are the prime models for us in a lifelong commitment of monogamous marriage.

Key marriage tip: The Christian home is a prime target for Satan and his minions. Be aware and keep in mutual prayer so you are stronger than he.

Key marriage tip: Try new things, go to different restaurant, different vacation destinations, wear different clothes, serve in your church or community together to keep things fresh and exciting. Your goal, in trying new things you learn new things about each other.

Key marriage tip: Marriages thrive when we both have the willingness to work together to commune and solve problems.

Key marriage tip: Assumptions make the good sitcom plotlines; they do not make good marriages!

Key marriage tip: Be in sync! You and your spouse must be on the same page on key theological and moral ideas.

Key marriage tip: Understand your differences! Celebrate them! Understand that you are two completely different people, different sex, different thinking, different upbringing, and different experiences. Be willing to respect where the other comes from. Be mature, be accepting and listen first, speak second.

Key marriage tip: Arguing? Have a disagreement? Have a commitment as to how you will respond and remember the Fruit of the Spirit. Do not raise your voice, do not use foul language, especially around kids, it is extremely destructive, and do not escalate it. Do not bring back the past. Do not belittle! Rather commit to a plan to hear each other, listen, work it out or wait when you are both in a place to listen. Have a commitment that it is safe to talk and share one another's feelings. Respect and treat them as God has treated you!

Key marriage tip: To talk about it, and listen more, must be the cornerstone of your marriage relationship. *You shall become one...*

Key marriage tip: When there is a problem or crises, deal with it by using facts, listening and love, as quickly as possible. Do not hide it, do not prolong it. Prolonged conflict does nobody any good. Deal with one problem at a time; do not escalate and throw other stuff in—nothing can be dealt with or resolved.

Key marriage tip: In good communication, do not assume. You need to verbalize, build trust and rapport, have no secrets, be transparent, be open and honest, and show the Fruit of the Spirit.

Key marriage tip: You must understand what God has said and called us to in marriage; read and know *God has called us to live in peace...in order that we might bear fruit for God.* Matthew 5:32; 19:9; Romans 7:1-4; 1 Corinthians 7:10-15.

Key marriage tip: Honor each other as who they are. Work on yourself to be a better you, the you God made you to be. Quality change is contagious!

Key marriage tip: Try to see your spouse as God does, as His child and His provision to you. When we see this, we see Christ and can better honor and cherish them.

Key marriage tip: Chores, responsibilities, house work, yard work and so forth can be daunting and a place of contention. Try to have appropriate responsibilities, so no one person is overburdened. And try to enjoy it, it is your home, make it home sweet home, comfortable and honoring.

Key marriage tip: The essential working component to keep any relationship functioning is the ability to lower one's pride in order to forgive. To keep a marriage not just functional, but vibrant, we must forgive, and we forgive as Christ has forgiven us—completely.

Key marriage tip: How you handle conflict will determine how your marriage and children will succeed or fail, whether you will have a dysfunctional or a loving home.

Key marriage tip: Beware that escalation will only harm yourself and your spouse and family. Rather, if you start to engage in these dysfunctions, calm down, walk away, and look to solve rather than hurt.

Key marriage tip: Control your pride! If you do this, you will be on the winning side of faith, life and harmony!

Key marriage tip: There is a connection to how we treat our spouse that goes deeper than we realize between how we treat others and how God responds to us, especially in a family situation.

Key marriage tip: The solution to strife is to stay away from judgments, seeking fault in others, avoiding put-downs, and focusing on goodness.

Key marriage tip: Do not threaten or intimidate or use foul language; your spouse is supposed to be your best friend. There is no place for foul langue in the home; patience, wisdom, tact and kind wit overrule vulgarity!

Key marriage tip: Do not become obsessed with winning; rather, be obsessed with real love and faith. We do not need to shock our loved ones; we need to point to the Love of Christ!

Key marriage tip: Real effective forgiveness takes work and time! It flows from a heart that is redeemed and satisfied by the Blood of the Lamb.

Key marriage tip: To understand forgiveness, we need to look to Christ, who forgave us when we did not earn or deserve it. We can have mercy upon our spouse and family so to cancel their debts as Christ did with us!

Key marriage tip: Let it go! You must practice forgiveness in grateful response to the awesome Truth that is Christ and so that you may be able to enjoy God's goodness. Top of the list: your spouse.

Key marriage tip: Control your pride! If you do this, then you will be on the winning side of faith, life, and harmony!

Key marriage tip: Do not be critical or use foul or disparaging language; people need to be lifted up, not torn down, for healthy relationships. If you do feel tempted to tear down, stop for 24 hours and see what happens.

Key marriage tip: When you forgive your loved one, you cut the cancer out of your relationship. If you do not forgive, your whole family will become malignant.

Key marriage tip: To properly forgive your loved one, give it over as if it never happened. You will be surprised that once you do this, you will feel the load lifted off you and you can rest in the comfort of the Lord.

Key marriage tip: Forgiveness does not change what was done in the past. Forgiveness will heal and help further your relationship with your spouse!

Key marriage tip: Give your spouse space. If they or you are in a 'mood,' back off and do not engage. Pray and wait for the right timing to have deep conversations. Remember, love is patient!

Key marriage tip: Be willing to cancel the betrayal!

Key marriage tip: Sixty percent of couples in marriage counseling, identify money as the major problem. Please, learn to control your money so it does not control you!

Key marriage tip: Make sure both of you know how money works. Have a good biblical concept on how to deal with budgeting and debt. Most conflicts in a marriage deal with finances! If you have an agreed-upon budget and you both are trustworthy in sticking to it, you have virtually eliminated a major source of conflict in many relationships.

Key marriage tip: Do not give to get; rather give to just give as Christ gave to you. Commit to the promise, "I will be more and do more," and see what happens.

Key marriage tip: We must not be afraid to find out what God's plan is and yield to it.

Key marriage tip: Our marriages are to be mirrored to the Kingdom of God, to God's Glory and His purpose. Surrender to His Lordship, surrender your family and assets, your wants and needs to His love and care, and be the proper steward that loves, cares, has faith and is effectual!

Key marriage tip: Talk about your day with one another and listen. Not every detail, like what pantyhose you buy or every detail at work, just commune and listen. If they do not understand what you are explaining, then share why this is important; restate it in a different way.

Key marriage tip: Selfishness will never make you happy, and you can't expect others to fulfill only what Christ can. Please do not expect your spouse to fulfill you; rather, seek how to be less self-centered and more centered on how to build your family up. Only then will you be more fulfilled and happy.

Key marriage tip: God calls us to "cleave," not leave. Be the glue that sticks one another together.

Key marriage tip: You must embrace good listening and communication. Just be willing to listen without speaking and care enough to love enough to make this happen. Good, lasting marriages are built on communication; divorce is the result of the breakdown of our hailing frequencies.

Key marriage tip: To create the effective triumphant marriage depends on our heart and will to put it into play. Just thinking about it or postponing it or waiting for the other to respond will not bring a good marriage.

Key marriage tip: There will be change! Anticipate change, prepare for change, realize life is always changing. This is good, what is wrong can be set right or just will be temporary. Life becomes an adventure as you grow. There are the stages of life, careers, moving, kids, aging, health, family, life and death, there will always be change, your spouse will change, so will you, beware, embrace it, be willing to adjust and you will triumph through it with your focus on Christ.

Key marriage tip: Talk about how you will handle disagreements and conflict, when you are not having a quarrel.

Key marriage tip: Seek Christ, place Him first and foremost in your life, and He will provide. Seek yourself, and you will be sad and lonely in so many ways! Remember that the heart of any healthy relationship is love and respect!

Key marriage tip: We are not to love money, but regard it only as a tool; we are to be content in Christ, for He will never leave or forsake us.

Key marriage tip: We are called to be careful of the love of money call to be, for while wealth and riches are not evil in and of themselves, they usually will become evil as they become our "god!"

Key marriage tip: If you just focus on your hurts and losses, you will not be able to focus on Christ and making a better marriage.

Key marriage tip: "I am sorry," are the pleasantest words you can ever say to simulate that connectives and restoration!

Key marriage tip: You do not need to live up to others expectations or what others want you to be. Focus on God's precepts and the Fruit He wants you to have.

Key marriage tip: How does our Lord call us to deal with the sin in others? With truthfulness and love!

Key marriage tip: For us to grow, we must surrender our will, desires, plans upon our Lord Jesus Christ. The municipal center of the Christian life is Jesus Christ (Colossians3:4).

Key marriage tip: Do not be jealous or always suspecting your spouse is up to no good.

Key marriage tip: Do not be controlling, give them room to grow and surprise you. If you have clear evidence of wrongdoing, remember Matthew 18, care enough to confront and bring a pastor or counselor if they refuse. Remember, love is at first trusting.

Key marriage tip: Be affectionate. Sex is good, but affection is what soothes, woos and embarrasses and grows the relationship. From sitting close, to hugs, to being more physical. If there are problems in this area, then get help. Ask your doctor about medications too if needed. Just do not just do sex, if so, you are not really being affectionate, rather being cold instead.

Key marriage tip: Your husband or wife should be your best friend and ally. It is ok to have other good friends, but your spouse should be number one. Share in your journey of life; build your friendship with them first and foremost. The key to this is, be a real friend first.

Key marriage tip: You will have disagreements and fights. That is OK! If you never have a disagreement something is very wrong. The key is to listen and have a plan.

Preventing Divorce Tips

Divorce-proof tip: Marriages that are in trouble tend not to pray together or communicate nor do they spend time together. When this happens, it is time to refocus and reboot and get help.

Divorce-proof tip: Have a disagreement or a problem to solve; then, listen to their position. Be kind!

Divorce-proof tip: Never say anything negative about your spouse in public! Misery does not like company, and you will get bad advice back. Remember to love and respect. Only talk to a trusted friend or qualified pastor or counselor, and let your spouse know about it, (unless there is abuse).

Divorce-proof tip: Never drop bombshells in public that you have not discussed previously with your spouse. Like, *I got a new job, and we are moving.* Not good! Discuss first, and then tell others.

Divorce-proof tip: Show interest. Put your newspaper, magazine, phone or smart electronic device down when you talk, out for dinner and so forth. Real life lived in the present always supersedes media and virtual life!

Divorce-proof tip: When you fight, and you will have disagreements and problems, you have to take a step back away from the emotions and ask yourself, is this important? Is my point important enough to hurt my family?

Divorce-proof tip: When you are fighting, remember you already lost. Focus on how to resolve it and listen.

Divorce-proof tip: Plan ahead your disagreements. That is, have a plan how to handle each others point of view when you disagree and do that when you are not disagreeing.

Divorce-proof tip: When we realize that marriage is not about me, *what I want, what my spouse can do for me*, then, we are moving up in our relationship and will get more out of it and be more content.

Divorce-proof tip: Major on the majors, don't major on the minors, i.e. it is more important that you pray together than how the house is organized. It is more important to practice love than what color you should paint the bathroom…

Divorce-proof tip: Give compliments, give kind words of affirmation, make them feel special, even when you do not feel like it. We all need to feel loved, give the love you want in return and it may happen.

Divorce-proof tip: Do not just criticize or always talk about yourself, refocus on being positive with your spouse.

Divorce-proof tip: Make your marriage a priority and work it as it is. Spend time, quality time, date nights, treat them with kindness and the Fruit of the Spirit.

Divorce-proof tip: Be romantic! Do not be boring! Remember the excitement when you first were dating and try to be that exciting person who is interested in your spouse. Try to create memorable moments, plan fun stuff, get away, do not always do the same old things.

Divorce-proof tip: If things get stale, then be stimulating, try a hobby together, volunteer somewhere together, find some fun together.

Divorce-proof tip: Do not flirt, period. It is not harmless! That is the prime gateway to affairs.

Divorce-proof tip: Do not confide with the opposite sex with any personal encounters or moments or anything your spouse would not approve of.

Divorce-proof tip: Do not linger with people of the opposite sex. Do your job with kindness, worship in a respectful mode; but, do not hang out, unless your spouse is there.

Divorce-proof tip: Develop healthy friendships with the same sex. Your spouse is not designed to fulfill your entire social life. Make friends, too. The secret to making friends is simple, be friendly and interested in them.

Divorce-proof tip: Watching pornography is not harmless like the movies and TV depict. It is extremely destructive to your mind's eye, and what you see is not even real. It will replace effectual reality with what is fleeting, and will sneak and snake its way into your relationship and cause havoc.

Divorce-proof tip: Do not do what your spouse would not approve of. Do not do what you do not want your spouse to do. This will help you make wiser choices.

Divorce-proof tip: Get help when you need it even if you do not want it. See a qualified counseling pastor or therapist. There is not shame is seeking help, it is what God wants you to do!

Divorce-proof tip: Remember, forgiveness as Christ has forgiven you!

Divorce-proof tip: Never use or say the word 'divorce,' or *it would be better if we never been married.*

A Final Tip

Key marriage tip: Yes, you can! We can apply the love and forgiveness Christ gave us. This will allow us to do more, each being a helpmate to the other while growing in maturity and raising good and healthy children who love God and life—all becoming a precious family that is the anchor of the community and civilization.

If you need a gentle touch to get this, remember when we place a period, God can and will place a comma!

In Christ, all that comes to us is for God's glory, purpose, and our good. (Romans 8:28). He seeks to bring us closer to Himself by His love, joy, and peace (Romans 5:1-5) that we may share His love with those around us to convey God's purpose for His people (John 17:20-24; Acts 2:24; 44-47).

APPENDIX II

The "*One Another*" Passages

Bible passages essential for us to understand and develop healthy relationships by knowing we are called to *One Another*:

- Love one another: John 13:34-35; 15:12, 17; Romans 12:10; 13:8; 14:13; 1 Thessalonians 3:12; 4:9; 2 Thessalonians 1:3; 1 Peter 1:22; 1 John 3:11, 3:22; 4:8; 23; 4:7, 11-12; 2 John 1: 5
- Serve one another: Galatians 5:13; 21; Philippians 2:3; 1 Peter 4:9; 5:5
- Accept one another: Romans 15:7, 14
- Strengthen one another: Romans 14:19
- Help one another: Hebrews 3:13; 10:24
- Encourage one another: Romans 14:19; 15:14; Colossians 3:16; 1 Thessalonians 5:11; Hebrews 3:13; 10:24-25
- Care for one another: Galatians 6:2
- Forgive one another: Ephesians 4:32; Colossians 3:13
- Submit to one another: Ephesians 5:21; 1 Peter 5:5
- Commit to one another: 1 John 3:16
- Build trust with one another: 1 John 1:7
- Be devoted to one another: Romans 12:10
- Be patient with one another: Ephesians 4:2; Colossians 3:13
- Be interested in one another: Philippians 2:4
- Be accountable to one another: Ephesians 5:21
- Confess to one another: James 5:16
- Live in harmony with one another: Romans 12:16

- Do not be conceited to one another: Romans 13:8
- Do not pass judgment to one another: Romans 14:13; 15:7
- Do not slander one another: James 4:11
- Instruct one another: Romans 16:16
- Greet one another: Romans 16:16; 1 Corinthians 1:10; 2 Corinthians 13:12
- Admonish one another: Romans 5:14; Colossians 3:16
- Spur one another on toward love and good deeds: Hebrews 10:24
- Meet with one another: Hebrews 10:25
- Agree with one another: 1 Corinthians 16:20
- Be concerned for one another: Hebrews 10:24
- Be humble to one another in love: Ephesians 4:2
- Be compassionate to one another: Ephesians 4:32
- Do not be consumed by one another Galatians 5:14-15
- Do not anger one another: Galatians 5:26
- Do not lie to one another: Colossians 3:9
- Do not grumble to one another: James 5:9
- Give preference to one another: Romans 12:10
- Be at peace with one another: Romans 12:18
- Sing to one another: Ephesians 5:19
- Be of the same mind to one another: Romans 12:16; 15:5
- Comfort one another: 1 Thessalonians 4:18; 5:11
- Be kind to one another: Ephesians 4:32
- Live in peace with one another: 1 Thessalonians 5:13
- Carry one another's burdens: Galatians 6:2

Be devoted to one another in love. Honor one another above yourselves. Romans 12:10

(Again, if you are in an abusive relationship, please seek qualified professional help. If you are in danger, immediately seek help and contact law enforcement.)

APPENDIX III

Personal and Family Budgeting Ideas

"Honor the Lord with your wealth, with the firstfruits of all your crops; then your barns will be filled to overflowing, and your vats will brim over with new wine." Proverbs 3:9-10

"Budget" can feel like a bad word, restrictive and difficult.

Instead of thinking of a budget as a negative thing, remember that a budget is simply a "game plan" or a financial plan. We need to have money to live in today's society. Because money is a necessary aspect, a tool that we need to create, apply, and follow the plan. In doing so, we can be wise stewards with what God has blessed us, and we can competently handle money, time and things—all gifted to us for the glory of Our Lord. A well-designed budget considers necessities, generosity, and desires and benefits everyone—you, your spouse, your family, your friends, even strangers!

This is what we need to do: Work on a budget. It is not hard to do, and it will make your life so much easier!

How do we do this? As I started in Chapter 18, you need to have a plan. This starts with a biblical concept of how to deal with your money and debt. First, know your total income (what comes in). Then, count all of your expenses (what goes out). The goal is to always make sure the income is greater than the expense. Kindly and honestly communicate with each other to make sure that you are both aware of the reality and work from there. Put the plan on paper and discuss it together. If you need a template for examples, go to crown.org or biblicalstewardship.net.

You are a money manager for God as it all belongs to Him, and we work for Him!

Money is many things. It can be a blessing or a curse, a tool or a hindrance, a solution or a problem. It is what it is by how we see it and use it. Think of your money problems as opportunities to be solved. See money as a tool to please Christ help your family, church, ministry, and others. Your budget is a clue as to what is important and what is not. If you are not helping to support your family first and your church to do the Lord's work, then what are you doing (Matthew 28:18-20)?

Our Decision-Making Process

Make sure you make healthy decisions based on the Word of God and the character of our Lord. Please do make decisions based on pride, personal agendas, and power trips. This is necessary if you are to effectively establish unifying goals, to anticipate and adapt to change, with two people who have completely different experiences and vision for what they want and have. Your goal is to be kind, encourage your spouse, and to ensure that what they bring inside is valuable, what they want is valid (within reason), and your goal is to budget money in accordance with Godly priorities.

You are to tell your money what to do, not just wonder where it went!

- First of all, do not be overwhelmed!
- What do you have coming in? Total all the net income for a month. If your income is sporadic, make an average out of the last 12 months.
- What do you have going out? Total all the bills—rent, mortgage, utilities, groceries, insurance, fuel, clothing, all spending no matter how small for a month. Try to carry a little notebook and write down all of your expenses for a month, and you will see how much actually goes out. Notice what you spend on those little purchases; it adds up quicky!
- What are the other resources will you need (time, money, people)?
- What problems will you face? How will you solve them?

Make sure to pay God first and yourself second by giving the first percentage to the Lord and a percentage for your savings. Allocate your monies to first food, shelter, other necessary bills, transportation, work and school expenses, medical expenses, debts, clothing, gifts, and, finally, entertainment. A good way to prioritize is to think of what is absolutely necessary (first) to what is absolutely frivolous (last). Write it out:

- Pray about this. Ask God to guide you, to give you wisdom and discernment, and let Him know that you realize you need His help in this. He will hear you, and He will help you. Our Lord wants you to be successful, and He works for the good in all who believe in Him. This is a promise, and it is true.

- Make the budget. Use one piece of paper. Much later, when you are ready, try a more complex plan or computer program.
- Set goals. Think of things that you will need or want— newer car, more education, college tuition for children, home repairs, a vacation. This is your carrot on a stick.
- List the most important fixed items first—God, rent or mortgage, utilities, groceries, insurance premiums, taxes, childcare expenses, and transportation costs. Allow for savings; then, list discretionary items like dining out, coffee, date nights, vacations, and gifts. (Goal: Have at least 2 months worth of income saved for emergencies. After you have met this goal, continue to save for retirement and those other things that you know you will need or want.)
- Pay off debt. Debt can be daunting. Try this plan to make debt manageable. Pay more than the minimum whenever possible. Pay your bills on time, but give more focus to one bill at a time, beginning with the smallest debt you owe. For instance, if you have one debt that is $400.00 with low interest and one debt that is $24000 with high interest, pay off the smaller debt first. Yes, the interest is low, but as soon as you pay it off, you'll have more to throw at the big debt. As soon as the smallest debt is paid, tackle the bigger debt and pay more than the minimum when possible. If you have debts that are rather equal in size, but have different interest rates, pay as much as you can on each with a focus on tackling the biggest interest rate first. As soon as that debt is settled, take that money and apply it the

next and so forth. This speeds up the process greatly
AND makes the process manageable.

- Finally, anticipate. Cars break down, teeth get cavities,
clothes wear out, pipes leak, premiums are due monthly
or every 6 months, etc. If you have a hard time keeping
track of things, write down those things you know will
happen and set extra savings aside for those things you
that you don't anticipate.

As you do these things, pay attention. Notice what is a
necessity and what is not needed. Know what is used, and
what is wasteful or wasted. For instance, if you go to the local
coffee place, realize that this is a delicious treat and luxury.
If you can afford this after you have met all the budget plans,
continue on. However, if you're trying to find more money to
meet your responsibilities, this daily treat is unnecessary and
wasteful. Even if the cup is only $2.00 a day, this can add to up
to $40 to $60.00 a month. However, that cup of morning elixir
could cost you between $80 and $300 a month alone! The
same is true with eating out a lot or buying your lunch each
day. Your coffee and dining habits can add up to a car payment!
So, think it through. Is it better to buy a good coffee maker and
make it yourself? If you're willing to eat fresh, homemade
meals, you might help your budget (and your health)! If you
have bigger purchases to think of, consider buying a good,
used car with under 60, 000 miles. With regular maintenance
and good care, this kind of car can last for years.

*"Do not wear yourself out to get rich; do not trust your
own cleverness. Cast but a glance at riches, and they are
gone, for they will surely sprout wings and fly off to the sky
like an eagle."* Proverbs 23:4-5

Write out your budget:

What do you have coming in (net income)?

List all incomes:

What do you have going out?

List all bills and expenses:

Where do you need to allocate your income?

What is your agreed amount for giving? To whom and or what?

What bills need to be paid each month? Every six months? Every year?

What will go to savings?

What will go to pay off debt?

What are the bills and expenses that you anticipate to come up?

Set goals for your future.

"Remember this: Whoever sows sparingly will also reap sparingly, and whoever sows generously will also reap generously." 2 Corinthians 9:6

APPENDIX IV

What about Divorce and Remarriage?

"It has been said, 'Anyone who divorces his wife must give her a certificate of divorce.' But I tell you that anyone who divorces his wife, except for sexual immorality, makes her the victim of adultery, and anyone who marries a divorced woman commits adultery." Matthew 5: 31-32

What do we do if a divorce is in the picture of our life?

Matthew 5: 31-32; 12:1-12; 19:1-12

Jesus answers the question of marriage, divorce and remarriage, as He challenges the religious establishment to move away from their presumptions and gives us a direct call for us all to take marriage <u>seriously</u>!

Jesus is the One who gives us marriage and is the One who can make and heal a marriage. The theme that Jesus presents us with is that marriage is sacred; it is God's plan that we succeed at it. To emphasize this, the passage is sandwiched in between the scriptural context of forgiveness and abundant possibilities. The point is, to succeed in relationships, especially marriage, we have to look to God's precepts and not our desires. Our desires will lead us astray. His way leads to happiness and contentment!

People in Jesus time wanted a quick and easy divorce just as many do today. Thus, Jesus warns us that our customs and practices may be popular and allowed, but they are not necessarily good. We must always look to the precepts of Scripture and not to what we think we want. Divorce is almost always the wrong solution to the problems we face. It indicates walking away from responsibility and God's call. It will only result in our becoming further lost from others and from God. As, God wants our hearts and minds centered on Him; then our determination will change, as will our behaviors and how we treat one another.

Do not be the one who runs away; rather, run to Christ as Lord!

First off, we have to understand that marriage is an institution designed by God. Marriage is a commitment ordained by God. It is a relationship built by God. Marriage is sacred and binding. Look at this: *one flesh.* It means an inseparable union. A husband and wife become synergistically tied to one another. Each becomes greater together rather than apart from one another. From the very moment of Creation, God intended marriage to be an enduring and monogamous union. When we divorce for trivial reasons outside what Scripture allows (unfaithfulness, abandonment, or abuse), we are outside of His will and plan, and that is not a good place to be (Matthew 5:31-32; 19:3-11; 1 Corinthians 7:10-17)!

- God's perfect plan, even in a corrupt culture, was always oneness and intimacy!
- God's perfect plan is that marriage be based on commitment (Genesis 2:19-25).
- Jesus calls us to make the most out of our marriage by serving Him and loving our spouse with our whole heart and mind.

We live in an age of easy divorce to such a point that we have (in the United States) "no-fault" divorce—you can end your marriage without stating a reason! This is nothing new; Jesus lived in such a time with similar "no-fault laws." What does Jesus say we are to do? Read Matthew 5: 31-32. He went way beyond any Rabbi or law at that time, and ours (in this time), by saying that divorce for any reason is wrong, and unlawful, except for unfaithfulness. In so doing, Jesus removes any doubt of how important marriage is. Jesus further tells us, in so many words, that divorce is actually treachery and betrayal, as it causes and even forces someone else to sin!

Consider that this was during a time when women were considered almost as property, and a man could (many did) divorce a woman and leave her destitute without a second thought or consequence to him. Of course this was against the Law of God for the Jews, nonetheless it was practiced. Added to this, adultery under the case law of the Pharisees and the Roman occupiers saw only the unfaithfulness of the women. Men could do as they saw fit. This was just as the Jews did in the time of the Judges, where *everyone did as they saw fit*, meaning as they liked, not what God has called. They looked to sin and ignored God's law and their responsibility for obedience. This nearly ruined the nation of Israel, and it did wipe out the Benjaminites. If we can see what a mess that was, perhaps it can help us place our focus on the principles that marriage is an exclusive commitment between a man and wife, with no grounds for separation unless heinous abuse is at work (Judges 20; Genesis 2:24; Malachi 2:10-17; Matthew 19:4-6).

What Is Jesus teaching us about Marriage, Divorce, and Remarriage?

(Genesis 1:23-28; 2:18-23; Ezra. 9-10; Neh. 13:23-27; Matthew 5: 31-32; 19:1-12; 1 Cor 7:2-9; 39; 2 Corinthians 6:14; Ephesians 5:21-33)

Jesus, for that time and ours, attacks the *status quo* of popular thinking and acceptance. Just because others are doing something, it is not OK that you do it! From God's perspective, marriage is for the mutual benefit and help of the man and the woman.

Jesus responds to the pious, fraudulent leaders of His day with an argument about their spiritual maturity, which was pale. The Israelites were allowed to divorce for trivial reasons because they were not mature enough to understand real effectual love and relationships. The rest of the community was required to take care of the woman when she was let go. This was also to create insult to the man who negated her. This method helped restrain divorce; only the most obtuse and socially deformed individual would divorce in a God-fearing Jewish culture. When the culture became corrupt by losing sight of God, as in Jesus' time, divorce became prevalent (Deuteronomy 24:1-4).

- Marriage means they complete each other.
- Marriage prevents sin.
- Christians must only marry other believers, or else it will cause deep division later on.
- Marriage is for procreation, but not exclusive to it. That means this is not the only reason for marriage.

Remember, the mandate in marriage is to love, then and now, is an extreme wakeup-call that commands the husband to thoroughly exhibit all of the qualities of Biblical character in his relationship with his wife. This designates a unbroken practice of action with love and respect all of the time, not just when we feel like it. As Christ loved the church, not *because it was holy, but in order to make it holy* (1 Corinthians 13:4-7)!

When considering marriage, we need to pray for guidance and truly consider the person someone who will be in relationship with us for the rest of our lives. The intended spouse should be complementary (not a twin necessarily) to us. Once we have found our complement, we are to love, respect, honor and cherish him/her. We must know that an enduring relationship requires commitment and effort. The beautiful thing about God's Amazing Grace is that even if we have chosen badly (due to impatience, lust, pride, wrong thinking, sin), we still have the opportunity for a great marriage! After all, there must have been some spark, something that got you together in the first place; this spark can be kindled into something glorious and joyful.

So, what about the *certificate of divorce*?

This means God hates divorce. It was only offered because of the immaturity and hardheartedness of the people, who refused to go God's way. However, in that *Certificate of Divorce,* the man was responsible to care and provide for her until she remarried (Deuteronomy 24:1-4; Malachi 2:16; Matthew 19:8).

In the practice of the Law, many Pharisees had focused on the idea that if they just gave a certificate of divorce, they could have, as many do today, a "no-fault," where one can get rid of their marital commitment for any reason, and still be OK in God's eyes. WRONG! They concluded divorce was permissible as long a 'Certificate of Divorce' was given, totally missing the point of the Law. (Other Rabbis taught as Jesus did.) They missed the point by placing the importance on the certificate, and not on the commitment, so Jesus challenges them, and their prideful hypocrisy (Deuteronomy 24:1-4; Jeremiah 3:1)!

In the challenge to Jesus, the Pharisees point was that the first husband could not take his wife back if he changed his mind, because the wife had become "defiled," as he caused her to commit sexual sin, and she would just compound it further! Paul said the Law bound a woman to her husband as long he lived. Jesus cleared the misconceptions the Pharisees had and simply stated: To divorce a woman for any reason, other than sexual immorality, would cause her to be defiled when she remarried (Leviticus 18:20 and Numbers 5:13,14; Matthew 19: 1-12; Romans 7:1-3)!

What about Paul? He said that if a Believer has been abandoned by their spouse, they are no longer bound to their marital commitment. There are times when one person may decide to have a divorce where their spouse can do nothing to prevent it. I believe this falls under this category of unfaithfulness (1 Corinthians 7:15).

Jesus tells us this is about *sexual immorality*, as in being unfaithful, and this will cause major distrust that may never be fully restored. However, keep this on the front burner of your mindset: Reconciliation is always preferable. Divorce is only a last resort, when no hope remains, when there is ongoing abuse and all options of reconciliation have been sought. Some teach that abuse fits in this category as it is indeed unfaithful (Matthew 19:8-9).

Can we *marry a divorced person?*

Jesus exposes the treachery of divorce, because when a man divorces his wife (or visa versa) for any cause other than sexual immorality or other Biblical reasons, they cause the other to commit the sin of adultery! That means it places the other person in a situation where they are likely to remarry and become defiled as in adultery (Malachi 2:13-16)!

When we file for a divorce against our spouse, it *causes them to commit sin.* This means when a partner renounces their marriage vows, it forces the other into a predicament. Even though in their eyes the marriage has ended, in God's eyes they are still married. This, in effect, causes the other person to commit adultery! In the matter, when we have so many divorced women and men in the church who did not divorce under Biblical reasons, we have to ask,

"What do we do?"

The Bible says, *"Whoever marries a divorced woman commits adultery".* So, does this mean they cannot remarry? (And of course' 'women' meaning person, not a gender thing.) Many teach this, and that would be Biblically correct. However, we have to remember God's grace, and forgiveness.

This is a complicated manner that requires solid Biblical counseling by a trained, qualified, pastoral Biblically-centered person. Each situation is unique, and requires understanding, encouragement, and healing.

At the same time, we have to understand the harmful effects that divorce creates that are passed on to many generations. Making divorce permissive (because it is popular and legal with "no-fault" arguments) is a reflection of society's immorality and loss of virtue. It does not negate the destruction of divorce, and sin that it is. It does not change the fact that God hates it!

If you love Christ as your Lord, you will respect His authority, and you will abide by His teaching.

Not your Will, but His Will be done! The church must teach the proper ways to build solid Christian relationships, and offer counseling and acceptance, or the statistics will keep climbing. We have to be on guard against the erosion of Biblical values, and damage to our beliefs and Biblical mindset (Psalm 123:3; Mark 4:19)!

The only Biblically acceptable grounds for divorce are sexual immorality or abandonment.

We all need to remember that God is a God of grace and forgiveness. However, remember also that even though we have grace, we will live with the destruction and effects that you have caused! True repentance requires that if you are in that adulterous association, you must stop it now! If you have found yourself in a sinful adulterous association, or have made mistakes, and even divorced, yes, there is hope in our Lord

(Proverbs 5:15-21; Matthew 19:11-12; 1 Corinthians 6:7-11; Colossians 3:18-21; 1 Peter 3:1-7)!

- The point is that marriage and divorce are never to be pursued carelessly or taken for granted! Jesus, also by this decree, liberates women, giving, and protecting their rights.
- God›s Word must always be our final court of arbitration for settling any and all arguments; if it is not, we build a house of straw on a foundation of sand!

Our life on earth is not our ultimate hope and reality. This is mainly a place to learn and grow. What we do or do not do here will echo throughout eternity and determine our place in the future with rewards or condemnation! Do not let the lust of your flesh rule your heart and rob you of your future. Rather, seek forgiveness, and safeguard your future actions! The good news of Grace is forgiveness of our sins. Make no mistake, beloved. Although you are forgiven, the destruction you caused will have lasting consequences. You may not be able to rebuild the relationships destroyed by the sin of adultery. For the unrepentant adulterer, there may be no hope. However, if they do repent, the hope of salvation in our Lord is still available—as He is for us all (1 Corinthians 6:7-11)!

APPENDIX V

What Does This Come Down To?

For in Christ all the fullness of the Deity lives in bodily form, and you have been given fullness in Christ, who is the head over every power and authority. Colossians 2:9-10

For Further Bible Study on what God has for us in Relationships.

(Also, please read the previous book, "The Field Guide to Healthy Relationships," by the author, Richard Krejcir)

Our relationship to God and our connections with others comes down to the fact that *I must die to my self will and put on His Will.* It is not just applying Scripture to my life, but applying my life to Scripture. When we do this, we are being the transformed Christian, impacting, loving, and encouraging.

- Jesus authority is ultimate (Ephesians 1:20-22; 1 Timothy 6:14-15; 1 Peter 3:22)!
- His authority is based on the fact that all things were made by Him, and for Him (Psalm 2:8; John 1:1-3; Hebrews 1:2, 6; Colossians 1:16).
- He is worthy to be worshiped (Hebrews 1:6; Revelation 1:5; 5:11-12; 7:9-10).
- He is our Redeemer, and we are purchased by His blood (Acts 20:28; Ephesians 1:7; 5:23; 1 Peter 1:18-19).
- He is the supreme, the head of the body of all Christians, of His Church (Colossians 1:18).

- Jesus sent His Spirit to guide us into the truth (John 16:12-13).
- We are called to teach others to observe all that He commanded (Matthew 28:20; John 13:20).

When we are doing the above then we will realize:

- I need to commit myself to Christ as LORD over all, and do this completely, with repentance, by faith and without doubt.
- I can take the *One Another* passages (see appendix or a concordance) seriously and reverently.
- I can reflect on God's call and plan for me.
- I can reflect and proceed with God's call for me in my relationships—past, present, and future.
- I can see my marriage as God's plan and provision, and that it needs my continual work, effort, and love, and that this is God's will—what He desires.
- I can submit myself to my spouse with respect and love him or her with honor unconditionally, humbly, honestly, and completely.
- I can commit to positive and active communication.
- I can admit my sin and failures.
- I can seek and ask forgiveness.
- My relationships will be edified, equipped, and empowered by what Christ has done for me and is working in me.
- I can renew my relationships through His empowering of me.
- I will be modeling and representing Christ, His character, and love in all that I do.

- My relationships will become healthier, and setbacks will be overcome.

Heal me, O LORD, and I will be healed; save me and I will be saved, for you are the one I praise. Jeremiah 17:14

A Biblical mindset lays a Biblical foundation for a life transformed and triumphant!

It is the realization that God loves us, He has a plan for us, and our relationships are important and foundational. Our lives are not happenstance; they are purposeful when we are in Him. The people in your life are the people God has brought you. Your husband or wife and whatever choice or circumstance that brought you together is your spouse and your responsibility; even if you married the wrong person, he or she is the right person now. We have to be willing to connect and make it work. We also need to persevere with our church members, coworkers, family, and friends.

By recognizing who He is, we can abide and build on His Rock.

By our obedience in faith, we may suffer temptations, trouble, persecution, setbacks, and condemnation from the world, and even from other Christians. It may seem our foundation has shifted by that constant beating, but He will remain steadfast in us unconditionally and even more powerful when we remain steadfast in our faith. Keep your faith real, valuable, and practical on His solid Rock. He will not leave you nor forsake you. So, let Him be the Rock-solid foundation of your life and your relationships!

APPENDIX VI

How to Build Your Faith

The man without the Spirit does not accept the things that come from the Spirit of God, for they are foolishness to him, and he cannot understand them, because they are spiritually discerned. The spiritual man makes judgments about all things, but he himself is not subject to any man's judgment. 1 Corinthians 2:14-15

How to Develop a Devotional Time (this also makes a 2 to 3 week Small Groups study)

Draw closer to the heart of God by building a deeper relationship with God!

Peter talks about humbleness, which is characterized by the willingness to grow in Christ, by which we receive learning, resulting in the experience of rational, emotional, and spiritual growth. Two of the best ways to do this is through personal devotional time and by being a part of a small group Bible study. Peter tells us we ought to be humble toward one another so that we can know the Grace of God and not be in opposition to God. Secondly, he says we had better be humble, not only toward one another, but toward God. This is so straightforward. It is so essential to become a blessed and growing Christian and church, not necessarily in numbers, but in what is most important—discipleship—which is leaning on, learning from, and growing in Christ, leading to a lifestyle of worship (2 Peter 1:5-7)!

How can I develop quality time with our Lord so I can become a deeper and more mature Christian?

Here are nine thoughts to get you pointed in the right direction:

1. **GOAL**: See where you are spiritually (Acts 22:8-10; Philippians 2:13) and determine where you need to go. Then, make a goal, and understand your GOAL. Your goal is to become complete, that is, finding fullness in Christ (Colossians 1: 28). To say it another way, it is to become a mature Christian, a person whose attitudes and actions are like Christ's (Ephesians 4: 13). Where are you spiritually and where do you need to go? Not only where do you want to go, but also where is God calling you to go?

2. **PROCESS**: Understand there is a process at work (Psalm 16:11; 73:28; Proverbs 16:9; Hebrews 11:1-6). It does not happen overnight, and you cannot get it in a bottle, off a shelf, or by sitting in a pew. The process is one of the main growth builders. It is about the journey as well as the destination. It is an essential step toward reaching your goal to spend personal, daily time with God. Thus, the journey is as important, if not more, than the destination, because in our walk, we are learning and growing. If we just arrived at the goal without the struggles of getting there, we would not have built any depth, strength, or maturity. Make sure your goals are a match to God's. We must never allow our presumptions and pride to cloud His way.

3. **PLAN:** Planning ahead (Isaiah 26:3; Mark 1:35) does not automatically happen. You need to plan out your devotions to make them more effective. You can get many prepared devotional schedules at a Christian bookstore or sit down on Sunday and decide exactly what paragraphs or chapters you will be studying during each of the next seven days. Doing this will eliminate the problem of spending half of your devotion time trying to decide what you will study that day. You can use a Bible reading chart, quality devotional books, or a pre-written guide, but try not to just dive in. You will get much more out of your experience by having a plan.

4. **CONTENT:** Put into your devotional time variety and consistency (Psalm 16:8-11) in what you study. One month, you might study an Epistle. Then, you might spend a month or two in a narrative passage such as 1 Samuel. Then, you might go back to the New Testament to study a doctrinal passage such as Romans. Then, switch again to a minor prophet such as Joel. Try to go through the entire Bible in your devotional study within a year, or two years at the most. Do not stay in just one section, such as the Epistles, and do not skip the Old Testament, as you cannot understand the New without the Old. Do not use the same plan year after year. Break it up, and try new ones. Do the same with your devotional books. Mix them up. If you have a good one such as *My Utmost for His Highest*, by Oswald Chambers, stick with it for the entire year, go to another one, and then go back to Chambers in the following year. When we are too consistent, it may turn into rhetoric, and then you will have a habit, not time with Christ!

5. **FOCUS:** Set aside time each day by focusing on the purpose for your growth and maturity (Psalm 119:130; Isaiah 42:16; John 4: 23-24; 15), and then **make it a priority.** In doing so, you will be able to "go for it" with passion and vigor. Let Christ transform you through His Word. ATTITUDE is essential. You must start with the proper attitude. You go before a Holy GOD! Usually, it is good to spend most of your devotional time closely examining a few verses, not rushing through multiple passages. This will help you keep focused. Some find it best to take notes and write down questions to ask a mentor about. In addition, you can set aside one day a week to switch from taking detailed notes on a few verses, to reading a chapter or two from a different passage without taking any notes. Whatever way you choose to go, stay focused and do not *bite off more than you can chew.*

6. **MATERIALS:** Get the best stuff you can get, and buy a good Bible (Ephesians 4:1-3) in an easily understood translation such as the *New Living Translation.* Consider using a Study Bible. I prefer *The Reformation Study Bible.* For serious study use the ESV (English Standard Version), NASB, NIV, or the NKJV. The best devotional books are *My Utmost for His Highest* by Chambers, and *Evening by Evening* by Spurgeon. You can also get a notebook that can be used exclusively for things that pertain to your relationship to God and to other believers so you can write down what you learn and any questions you may have.

7. **PLACE OR LOCATION:** Select a quiet place (Luke 5:16) to study where you are free from distractions. Remove all distractions. Close the drapes, shut the

door, turn off the TV and radio, clear all busy work from your desk, take the phone off the hook, and lock the cat in the bathroom—whatever it takes. You will then be better able to concentrate and have quality time with Him. Be serious about meeting God!

8. **TIME:** Select a quality time (Ephesians 2:18). Chose a time for your devotions when you are at your best. Usually, early morning is best, because outside distractions are at a minimum during this time. If you are not a morning person, do it when you are most alert. Give God your best. Set aside "x" number of minutes to study, and "y" number of minutes to pray. Be flexible to the Spirit's leading within this framework. If you have a short attention span (as I do), then break it up throughout the day. Perhaps read from the Old Testament in the morning, a passage from the New Testament at lunch, then read a devotion and practice intercessory prayer before bedtime. Remember, this time is holy, which means it is to be set apart to and for God only. If you are just being devoted to your plan and time, then there will be little room for Christ. The plan is the tool for growth, not the growth itself.

9. **SHARE** what you have learned (Psalm 55:14; Matthew 18:20; Romans 12; 2 Corinthians 12:18). We learn by doing and sharing. What we have been given is usually not meant for us solely; it is a gift that keeps on giving as we, in turn, help others. A willing heart, a teachable spirit, and the willingness and availability to share are essential for a disciple of our Lord!

From these nine precepts, we realize that from the character of Christ comes the conduct of Christ, if we choose to follow

Him. Those values of our daily walk that drive our behaviors will, in turn, influence others and build our character. You cannot lead where you have not been or when you do not know the direction to go. This is why discipleship is so essential to the aspect of being a Christian. We are called not just to visualize discipleship, but to do it—not just to talk about it, but to do it. One cannot just think about dinner and satisfy hunger. The ingredients need to be gathered, the meal has to be prepared. Only then is it eaten. The Christian who wants to go deeper and become more mature, as well as the effective church, will take Scripture and the call of our Lord seriously, and implement it and apply it to their lives.

APPLICATIONS: Here are some thoughts to consider about applying and turning your devotional time into action.

1. You will never be able to fully experience the value of a devotional time until you discipline yourself to apply what you have learned. Study with the determination that God will give you an application. Then, be willing and able to put it into action without fear or trepidation. Allow your trust in Christ be real and exercised!
2. Make your applications measurable. Think through the *who, what, where, when, how* and *why,* such as *I will begin showing more love to my neighbor by asking if there is anything I can pick up for them from the store next time I go shopping.*
3. Sometimes, you will see four or five specific ways the passage you have studied can be applied. It is better to select one you want to apply from the Word that day and do it. If you try to implement three or more ways, you will most likely get frustrated and fail. If you

cannot decide, stick to the first one that pops up or one in the area where you need the most help.

4. Make most of your applications short-ranged, such as things you will do within the next day or so, or within the week. Periodically, God will give you an application that you will need to work on for a longer time. When that happens, rejoice and praise God, for this will build you up. At the same time, continue to work on fresh, short-range applications. See them as baby steps that will eventually turn into a marathon. Let God do a new work in you each day, and be thankful He wants to work in you.

When we are growing, we become contagious with the faith. We then are able to witness because we have something to say and something to model that people want. When we are growing, we will become the church that Christ designed, mobilized in Him to be welcoming and connectedness to others for Him. This is the church triumphant! Let us, as the church triumphant, pay heed to His call and follow it. Apply your faith. Then, watch your faith grow and become contagious to others!

Conclusion:

There are many ways we can do devotions and study the Bible effectively. There is no "best" way, only that we do it. Many Christians feel all they have to do for their spiritual growth is sitting in a pew, turn on the television or radio, or naturally receive knowledge just by being a Christian. However, this is not the way to transform our lives. We can no better grow deeper in Christ without any effort as we could go to a grocery store, stand in the produce section, and become a cucumber. To be a mature and growing Christian, we must read and get into the Word of God ourselves. We do it through prayer, hard work, discipline, concentration, application, and even more **prayer!**

Take this to heart: Jesus never asked anyone to do anything without enabling them with the power to do it. Let this be your encouraging motive (Matthew 28:20)!

Remember, Christ loves you, and wants the best for you. His way is the best way, and we need to have Him and the perspective of eternity in mind, removing the focus from our limited feelings and desires.

Discussion Questions:

1. How can I develop quality time with our Lord so I can become a deeper and more mature Christian?
2. Has your passion and zeal for witnessing grown or diminished over the years? What were the reasons?
3. What causes bitterness in people? How does bitterness come into play when you witness?
4. What are the distinctions, character, and personality of a Christian who bases all his or her life, IT ALL, upon Christ, with full trust and assurance by faith and obedience? What would this do to evangelism efforts?
5. How do we get to be righteous? What is the key ingredient?
6. Christians receive the gift of Grace, but do not give the gift to themselves. How does it make you feel to know that you cannot earn or buy God's most precious gift?

7. Take a close look at who in your life, at work, school, at the shoe store, or wherever has not confessed Jesus as Lord? How can you bring the message of the most precious Gospel to them?

8. Jesus comes as the good Shepherd to rescue His lost sheep. How are you, or how could you be, comforted with this truth?

9. What are you focused on? Is it money, job, family, hobbies, food? How is your focus related to God's focus?

10. When you are putting your faith into practice, how do you feel when people reject you or treat you badly?

11. What holds you back from embracing God's call to you?

12. How much does fear affect your motivation to be involved in a ministry?

Some passages to consider on discipleship and mentoring which are not options, but a command: Proverbs 18:24; Matthew 7:18-24; 10:1-42; 19:28-30; 28:16-20; Mark 1:1-5; 1:35-2:12; Luke 9:23-25; 48; Luke 14:26-27; John. 8:31; 12:20-26; John 14; 15; 1 John: 5:3; Romans 12; 1 Corinthians 3:5-11; 12; Galatians 6:1-10; 2 Timothy 2:7; 1 Peter 3:15.

More tools on Discipleship are available at www.intothyword.org, www.withtheword.org and www.discipleshiptools.org

APPENDIX VII

Index of Scriptural Passages

For further insights from God's Word, go over each of these Bible passages using the inductive questions below:

1. What does this passage say?
2. What does this passage mean?
3. What is God telling me?
4. How am I encouraged and strengthened?
5. Is there a sin in my life for which confession and repentance is needed?
6. How can I be changed so I can learn and grow?
7. What is in the way of these precepts affecting me? What is in the way of my listening to God?
8. How does this apply to me? What will I do about it?
9. What can I model and teach?
10. What does God want me to share with someone?

For even a deeper study, see the book *Into Thy Word: How to Do An Inductive Bible Study* by the author, Richard Krejcir. The book is available at Amazon or at intothyword.org along with a downloadable "Chart" and "Cheat Sheet" with all the tools you need to take these Scriptures and study them in-depth in your personal devotions or lead others to do so in your teaching, Bible study, or sermons!

The Journey of Love and Relationships: Numbers 6:24-26; Joshua 1:8; Psalm 32:8; 119:9, 24; Proverbs 6:22-23; 12:4;

28:20; 31:10; **Mark 12:30-31;** John 8:31-32; Colossians 1:3-6; 2 Timothy 3:16-17; 2 Peter 1:4

Prime Marriage Passages: Proverbs 3. Malachi 2:14-16; Matthew 19:6; 22:1-22; Luke 16:18; John 13:34-35; Ephesians 5:15-16; 1 Corinthians 7:1-11, 39-40, 13:1-13; Ephesians 5:25-27; Colossians 3:12-14; Hebrews 13:4; James 4:1-3

How to build a Great Marriage: Mark 12:30-31; John, chaps 14-15; Ephesians 4:29-32; 5:1-33; 1 Peter 3: 1-12

More Marriage passages to consider: Psalm 32; 51; 1 Corinthians 7:32-35; 13; 2 Corinthians 1:39; Galatians 2:20-21; Philippians 1:6; 3:10; Colossians 2:2, 3:15-17; 1 Thessalonians 5:23-24;

God's Care: Leviticus 19:18; Psalm 37:4; 139:13-16; Proverbs 23:7; 27:19; 28:26; Jeremiah 17:9; 29:11; Matthew 6:25-34; 10:31; 15:19; John chaps14-15; 17:25-26; Romans 5:8; 2 Corinthians 5:7-9; 5:14-20; Ephesians 1:3-4; 2:4-9

Love: Deuteronomy 6:5; Matthew 22:37-40; Mark 12:30-31; Luke 10:27; John 13:34-35; 15:12, 17; Romans 12:10; 13:8; 14:13; 1 Corinthians 13; Ephesians 5:15-18; 1 Thessalonians 3:12; 4:9-12; 2 Thessalonians 1:3; 1 Timothy 1:15; James 3:8-10; 1 Peter 1:17, 22; 1 John 3:11, 3:22; 4:8; 23; 4:7, 11-12; 1 John 4:8; 2 John 1: 5

Cherish, Submission and Respect: Deuteronomy 22:6; Proverbs 4:2-9; 19:8; Romans 2:11; Galatians 2:6; Ephesians 4:29-32; 5:1-33; Colossians 3:18-19; 1 Thessalonians 2:6-8; 4:9-12; James 2:1,9; 1 Peter2: 17; 3:8-9, 18-4:1, 5:6-7

Forgiveness: Psalm 32; Matthew 18:21-35; Luke 23:34; **Ephesians 4:32;** Colossians 3:13

Communication: Proverbs 29:20; Matthew 21:22; Luke 8:18; John 8:47; Romans 12:10; Galatians 5:22-23; Ephesians 4:15, 25-29; Colossians 3:5,16, 4:6; 1 Timothy 4:12; James 1:19-25; 1 Peter 3

Mature Christian: Acts 2:4; 4:8, 31; 6:3; Romans 8:9; 1 Corinthians 7:32-35; 12:13; Ephesians 5:8-6:9, Colossians 3:19-4:1

Put off Sin: Psalm 103:12; Isaiah 43:25; Mark 1:5; Acts 7:58; Romans 13:12-14; Ephesians 4:24-25; 1 Peter2:1

Relationship Breakdown: Proverbs 13:10-12; Matthew 5: 1-12; John 16:33; Acts 20:31; Romans 6:11; 15:5-7; 1 Corinthians 12:26; 2 Corinthians 2:1-4; 4:6; 5:2, 12; 10:17-18; Galatians 6:1-8; Ephesians 1:3-7; 4: 2, 11-16, 25-32; Colossians 2:13,14; Ephesians 1:3-5; 4:2, 11-15; 26; 1 Thessalonians 2:7-8; James 1:9-10, 19; 4:1-11, 29; 1 Peter 1:22-2:10; 4:7-11; 29; 5:5

Conflict: Proverbs 13:10; 17:14; 28:13; Matthew 5:32; 15:19; Luke 15:11-24; John 17:20-23; Romans 7:1-4; 12:9-21; 1 Corinthians 6:1-8; 7:10-15; 13:5; **2 Corinthians 12:9-10;** Philippians 1:27-28; Colossians 3:12-14; James 1:19-25; 1 John 1:8-9

Scriptural helps: How to Destroy a Relationship: John 3:5; Romans 3:23; 1 Corinthians 4:6; 5:2; 13:4; 2 Corinthians

5:12; 10:17-18; Galatians 6:1-5; Colossians 1:18; 2 Timothy 3:2-5; James 1:9-10; 4: 1-6 ; 1 Peter 5:5; Revelation 3:17

Pride: Job 35:12-13; 40:12; 41:34; 2 Chronicles 26:16; 32:26; Psalm 10:4-5; 18:27; 31:18; 56:2; 59:12; 62:10; 73:6-12; 101:5; 119:21; 131:1; 6:17; Proverbs 3:34; 8:13; 11:2; 13:10; 16:5,18; 17:4; 21:4; 24; 27:2; 28:25-26; 29:23; 30:13; Isaiah 2:11-21; 5:21; 13:19; 16: 6; 23:9; Ezekiel 28:2; Obadiah 1:3; Habakkuk 2:4; Mark 9:35; Luke 16:15; John 5:44; Romans 1:21-32; 12:16;1 Corinthians 1:6; 2 Corinthians 5:12; 7:4; Galatians 6:4 and these are just a few!

Defensive Mechanisms: Proverbs 17:4; Matthew 7:1-5; 21-23; 25:31-33; Luke 15:17-19; John 5:22

Defensiveness: Proverbs 17:14; John. 3:5; 13:34, 35; Ephesians 4:15; 2 Timothy 2:23-24; 4:1-2; 1 Peter 5:5

Contempt: Psalm 94:4; 18:25-26; 62:12; Proverbs 27:15; 29:9; Matthew 7:1-5; John 5:24; 16:33; Romans 2: 1-16; 1 Corinthians 3:18; 4:17; 2 Timothy 2:22-26; 2 Peter 2:10

Criticism: 2 Samuel 6:20; Psalm 15; Proverbs 17:27-28; 26:18-20; Philippians 2:3-6; James 3:13-4:2

Withdraw: Matthew 5: 13-16; John 1:15; 16:33; Galatians 6; Colossians 1:13; James 1:5-8; 1 Peter 2:9

Getting Over It: Job. 23:10; 36:5; Psalm 19:12-14; 139:23-24; Proverbs 25:15; Jeremiah 17:9-10; Romans 5:3-5; 1 Corinthians 12:26; 13:4-8; 2 Corinthians 2:1-4; Galatians 6:3-5; Ephesians 4:15, 32; 5:1-2. 28-29; Philippians 1:27-30;

1 Thessalonians 5:16-18; Ephesians 4:31-32; Hebrews 12:15; 1 Peter 2:17, 3: 7

Disappointments: Psalm 136; 142:1-7; Proverbs 3:5-6; 20:30; 23:10; Isaiah 26:3; Matthew 6:33; 21:21-22; John 7:17-18; Romans 8:28-29; 2 Corinthians 1:9; 4:7-12; Philippians 1:27-28; James 1:4-8; 1 Peter 1:6-7

Getting over Hurts: Exodus 23:4-5; Leviticus 19:17-18; Psalm 19:12-13; 25:21-22; Proverbs 3:5; 16:32; 25:28; Romans 13:11-14; Galatians 5:22-23; Ephesians 4:26-27; Philippians 4:6-7; Tim. 2:22, Hebrews 12:2, 15; 13:4; 2 Peter 1:5-7; 5:6-7

Money and marriage: Psalm 24:1; Proverbs 1:7; 3:5, 9-10; Matthew 6: 19-24, 33; 7:24-27; 19: 16-26; Luke 12:33-34; 1 Corinthians 4:2; 2 Corinthians 9:6-15; Ephesians 5:15-16; 1 Timothy 6:9-19; Hebrews 10:32-39; 13:5; 1 Peter1:3-5; 1 John 5:21

Divorce-proofing your marriage: Genesis 2:24; Proverbs 3:1-35; 6:26-33; 7:24-28; 18:13; Malachi 2:14-16; Matthew 5:12, 5:27-28; 19:6; Luke 16:18; 1 Corinthians 6:9; 16-18; Ephesians 5:15-16; Hebrews 13:4; James 1:19; 4:1-3; Revelation 21:2

Building Healthy Relationships: Genesis 4:4-7; Psalm 23:4; 27:1-14; Proverbs 1:7; 3:3-10; 12:25, 28; 25:15; Isaiah 1:10-15; Jeremiah 6: 20; Amos 5:21-24; Matthew 5:11-12; John 3:5; 8:12; 1 Corinthians 3:16-17; 10:23-24; 2 Corinthians 3:16-17; 4:6; 9:12-13; Ephesians 4:15, 5:8-9; Philippians

1:27-30; 2:3-8, 14-15; Colossians 4:6; Hebrews 11:6; James 1:17;1 Peter 1:22-23; 2:9-12, 21-27; 1 John 4:7-12

Forgiveness: Exodus 34:6-7; Isaiah 55:8-9; Psalm 32; Proverbs 10:12; Matthew 18:21-35; Luke 6:27-31; 23:34; John 13:34-35; Romans 12:2; 2 Corinthians 7:8-11; **Ephesians 4:29-32;** Colossians 3:12-14; 1 Peter 2:23-24; 4:7-8

Confidence and trust in the Lord: Deuteronomy 31:6-8; Psalm 56:11; 118:6; Philippians 4:11-12; Hebrews 2:15; 4:16; 11:23, 27

What Does This Come Down To Passages: Genesis 1:26-27; 2:18-24; Deuteronomy 4:9-10; 5:29; 31:11-13; Judges 2:6-13; Jeremiah 17:14; Psalm 2:8; 78:5-8; 127:1; Matthew 16:24; 28:20; Luke 9:23; John 1:1-3; 3:30; 13:20; 16:12-13; Acts 20:28; Romans 7:4, 18; 1 Corinthians 3:11; 10:4; 2 Corinthians 11:2; Galatians 2:20; Ephesians 1:7, 20-22; 2:20; 5:23; Colossians 1:16-18; 2:4-10; 1 Timothy 6:14-15; Hebrews 1:2,6; 13:5; 1 Peter 1:18-19; 3:22; Revelation 1:5; 5:11-12; 7:9-10

Marriage Tune-up: Deuteronomy 31:6-8; Jos. 1:5; 2 Chron. 15:2; Psalm 37:28; 86; Malachi 2:14-16; **Matthew 6:19-34; 19:6;** 16-26; Luke 12:15, 21; 16:18; 1 Corinthians 7:3-5; 13:4-7; Hebrews 13:4. Ephesians 5:20-33; Philippians 1:6; 4:10-13; Colossians 3:15-17; 1 Timothy 3:3; 6:6-19; 1 Peter 1:3-5; 2:1-12; 3: 1-12

Epilogue: Hebrews 3:12-13; 4:1-2; 5:11-6:3; James 1:22-25

He must become greater; I must become less. John 3:30

APPENDIX VIII

Helpful Links and Further Marriage Resources

Homeward, Jim Burns, a site filled with great resources: www.homeword.com

Family Life—Help and Hope for Marriages: *www. familylife.com*

Focus on the Family: www.family.org

What the Bible says about relationships: www.intothyword. org/pages.asp?pageid=53504

Resources for a Bible Based Christian 12 Step Recovery

www.churchleadership.org/pages.asp?pageid=67284

www.discipleshiptools.org/pages.asp?pageid=65408

Discipleship:

InterVarsity: www.intervarsity.org
Discipleship Tools: www.discipleshiptools.org
With The Word: www.withtheword.org
Into Thy Word Ministries: www.intothyword.org
Monergism: www.monergism.com

Recovery Groups:

Rapha: www.rapha.info
Desert Stream Ministries: www.desertstream.org
http://www.newlife.com
http://www.raphacare.com

Prayer:

Mission America: www.missionamerica.org
Harvest Prayer Ministries: www.harvestprayer.com
The Upper Room: www.upperroom.org

Myers Briggs

http://myersbriggs.org

EPILOGUE

The solution to a great marriage is the willingness to live life as one who has encountered Christ and play it forward as an encourager to our family!

If you want to be successful in your marriage, you need to "get it"—know and work on real love, cherishing and respecting. By this, we create the happy home that glorifies and serves God. Our desires and pleasures are not God's priority for our lives; God is our priority, and we are to follow His lead into your marriages!

Yes, God wants us to be joyful, happy, and content; however, being happy means focusing on Him and not on our circumstances. To have a successful marriage, you must be aware of what you are getting into and prepare for it. The most important guarantee for it to work is to follow His principles from His Word, not what you think, want, or have experienced. Remember, God designed marriage and us. He knows best (Colossians3:18-19; Ephesians 5:21-27; James 4:7-8; 1 Peter5:5)!

How will this book help me if I am not a Christian? The tips and principles in this book are called 'precepts'—timeless Truth. These precepts are in the Bible; the Bible is God's Truth. The precepts are found in real research—scientific truth. The precepts are shown to be effective far beyond counseling—societal and cultural truth.

If one of you does not embrace any of which we have talked about so far, you will have an extreme strain on your relationship, and you face the odds of a 50% divorce rate. Of the marriages that are left, from my experiences in counseling and research, most are miserable! Please, please consider how important it is to *get your act together; you* have already said, "I do!"

He who covers over an offense promotes love, but whoever repeats the matter separates close friends. Proverbs 17:9

Hebrews 3:12-13; 4:1-2; 5:11-6:3; James 1:22-25

The real authenticity of our Lord, will enable us to build a real authenticity of love and respect, that will in turn build a "Wondrous Marriage!"

God desires us to be transformed agents of His Work and Word!

The Author, Richard Joseph Krejcir is the cofounder and Director of *Into Thy Word Ministries*, a missions and discipling ministry. He is the author of several books, including *Into Thy Word*, *A Field Guide to Healthy Relationships* and *Network*. He is also a pastor, counselor, researcher, and speaker. He is a graduate of Fuller Theological Seminary in Pasadena, California (M.Div.) and holds a Doctor of Philosophy in Practical Theology from London (Ph.D). He has garnered over 30 years of pastoral ministry experience, including serving as an Equipper of Pastors, Church Planter and Church Growth Consultant.

The LORD bless you and keep you; the LORD make his face shine upon you and be gracious to you; the LORD turn his face toward you and give you peace. Numbers 6:24-26